BY AL PALMQUIST
with Joyce Hovelsrud

HOLY SMOKIES
The Real Centurions

 Minneapolis, Minnesota

ARK BOOKS

(Owned and operated by MIDWEST CHALLENGE, INC.)

COVER ART:
David Stone

COVER PHOTO:
Ake Lundberg

Ark Books
Copyright © 1977

ISBN 0-934400-07-5

Printed in the United States of America

Foreword

When a man of faith dares to stand in the streets of a large city where criminals lurk and lawlessness abounds, when he dares proclaim to those he encounters that Jesus Christ is the way of salvation for all men, miracles are going to happen.

Police Officer Al Palmquist is such a man who dares. In the midst of violence and crime, Al clothes himself with the armor of God, arms himself with the Word, and patrols his city as a true centurion.

This is the story of the amazing way in which God revealed His plan to one police officer. This is a story of miracles ... of a "Christ-centered program so effective in rehabilitating devastated lives that law officers are beginning to catch the vision" and adopt different methods of dealing with crime in the streets. It is a dramatic story of changed lives.

I first met Al Palmquist in 1973 when he was assigned to my Team for security during one of our crusades in Minneapolis. I rode in his squad and caught a glimpse of the awesome responsibilities that rest with those who enforce the law and protect our society from those who would destroy it. He gave his testimony at one of the meetings during that crusade and some 30,000 people thrilled to hear the story of his mission.

4

Al is a man of profound faith and courage, a man of compassion for his fellow man, and a man of conviction that their needs must be met through the saving power of Jesus Christ. He is a man of determination and action.

Through the pages of this unique book, God speaks to those in positions of authority. He speaks to parents and to young people. He speaks to all who have experienced emotions of bitterness, loneliness and despair and to those who have become hopelessly ensnared in the insidious web of lawlessness and sin.

This is a book which gives clear-cut answers to perplexing questions and presents tangible solutions to desperate problems.

I praise God this story has been told, and I heartily and prayerfully recommend the reading of it.

Billy Graham

Chapter I

The Message

I used to think baseball was one of the four seasons in Minnesota where I grew up. It followed winter. As soon as the first trickle of a spring thaw would come, I'd dash to the nearest ball park and play from dawn to dusk. Then I'd drop into bed planning more of the same for the next day. I never got tired of the schedule.

Winter was different. While I enjoyed such outdoor sports as skating and tobogganing when the first snows came, I lost all interest in them along toward baseball time and I'd get to where I couldn't stand another snowfall. I'd sit inside deploring my lack of adventure and trying my mother's patience asking, "What can I do?"

Today I find plenty of adventure when cold snows cover the city of Minneapolis. Something interesting always happens. Each day is packed with action. Some of it lifts the heart. Some if it sickens the soul. All of it adds a variety and challenge I wouldn't trade for all the baseball games of my childhood.

I'm a cop.

I'm also a preacher.

How that seemingly strange combination came about, I'll explain later; but I'll state at this point I don't consider combining those two vocations unusual at all.

In my business, there arise many occasions which call for words to be said—words of counsel, words of comfort, words of hope. Often it's difficult to find the right ones . . . even with all my experience behind a pulpit; for now the members of *my* congregation don't sit comfortably in pews and listen to inspirational messages without frightening interruptions.

They lie on the highways dying from jagged wounds.

They walk handcuffed toward prison cells where confinement behind cold steel bars awaits them.

They clutch stolen goods and run in fear from pursuing police officers carrying guns.

They crouch in dingy rooms and shoot deadly drugs, hoping their "highs" will lift them from the depths of misery.

They cry in the streets looking for a lost dog, or maybe for a mom or a dad.

Every now and then, however, something comes along to add a moment of hilarity to the seriousness of it all.

One sub-zero January night when angry winds whipped gusts of snow about the city, my partner Don and I were assigned a midnight watch. The streets were deserted save for other cops in squad cars. Even the crooks knew better than to be out in such weather. I was uneasy . . . not because I sensed something ominous about the night, but because I didn't like wasting time on the job. I liked action—plenty of it and this beat promised to drag on interminably without it.

"Wait . . . just . . . a . . . minute," Don said, slow-ing down the car and looking intently to his left. "You see that?"

I sat erect and scanned the scene. "All I see are tire tracks," I said with obvious disinterest. "So?"

"So we follow 'em," my partner said.

"Oh sure. Tire tracks on a snowy street are bound to spell trouble," I said, trying to stifle a laugh which quickly converted to a loud guffaw.

"I'm going to ask the Chief if he can get you on with the Keystone Cops," Don said wryly, then proceeded with Mission Tire Tracks.

They led us into an alley. "Aha," my associate continued with I-told-you-so connotations, "Super Sleuth will now show Funny Boy what cop business is all about."

As we approached a vacant warehouse, I began to think Don might have something after all. Once on a tip, we'd searched this particular building, found stashes of drugs, and subsequently located the pushers who'd been storing them there. It seemed logical to assume other pushers could be using the warehouse now, thinking it would be the last place cops would look since they'd done such a thorough cleaning on it once.

I braced myself for action. We stopped. Sure enough, two sets of footprints led to the door, two sets led from it. "They've been here and gone," I said. "Let's find them first, then we'll check the building."

"Right thinking," Don said as we got into the car and continued up the alley. I was dead serious now.

Our map in the snow took us on a circuitous route indeed. Around one block, through a second alley, around another block, and then . . .

"There's a car parked in front of that shack to

the right," I said. "Motor's running."

Don turned off the lights and stopped the car. "Let's hoof it from here," he said. "I'll radio a back up unit and cover you."

I slid from the squad. Half standing, half crouching, I eased my way toward what looked like big trouble. My muscles tensed as a door to the suspect car opened slowly. In the light dimmed by gusting snow, I could barely discern two figures. One turned toward me and shouted, "Hey, Palmquist, take us alive and I'll get you a promotion."

I recognized both men and vehicle at the same time: juvenile officers in Squad 851.

"You and your bright ideas," I said to Don as I got back into the car. He looked chagrined, managed an apologetic smile and slid over my direction, motioning for me to walk around to the driver's side.

"You steer this wagon to some excitement," he muttered and settled down for a snooze.

As I maneuvered about in the drifting snow, I tried to think of appropriate come-backs to counteract the razzing we'd get back at the station. I knew the guys in the juvenile squad would tell the story of my creeping up for the capture with an exaggerated flair. They always branched out into fiction when they ran out of facts while reporting cop boners. War stories, we called such reports.

Don invariably fell asleep when I drove the last hours of night duty so there was no conversation to keep me awake. But no matter. He snored at such full volume I couldn't have dozed if I'd taken a shelf full of sleeping pills.

Morning finally came and I headed for the Bryant Avenue Station.

"Hey, you snoring Sherlock, wake up."

There was no response. I hit him. I pinched him. I blew in his ear. He twitched and kept on snoring.

I rolled down the window and grabbed a handful of snow. Splat! Right in the old kisser. I reached for a second handful when Don grabbed my arm and twisted it until I dropped the ingredient intended for his second facial. "You big Irish jerk," he said, half laughing, half screeching. "If you weren't a preacher, I'd call you names that would burn your holy ears to a crisp."

Our fooling around came to a halt when the shouts and whistles of some twenty-five cops met our ears. The men emerged from the station and from squad cars to congregate in the street. Then what to our wondering eyes should appear but a middle-aged man prancing down the street toward us. Ordinarily we'd have been suspicious . . . at least curious, but in this circumstance, we were dumbfounded. It was 7 a.m., it was 20° below, and save for a pair of bedroom slippers, the man was nude! Now seeing may be believing, but not in *this* instance.

"Whaddya call a case like this?" one officer asked.

"Indecent exposure?" ventured a rookie.

"In *this* weather I'd call it *double* exposure," said another.

The crowd laughed. It was hilarious, I had to admit. But it was sad, too. "What do you say to a guy like that?" I whispered to Don.

"I don't know," he replied and Don was good in talking to people.

"He belongs in a rubber room," one officer said. "He's nuts."

"He's sick," I thought as I walked to the station. But how could I help him? Police Academy never prepared me for a case like this. Three years of Bible School and several counseling courses never taught me what to say to a nude running the streets in mid January. In four years of working with Teen

Challenge in New York City I'd never been faced with this sort of thing. I had no answer.

Not one of those twenty-five professional police officers had an answer. I was troubled. If the man had carried a cardboard sign that said I NEED HELP, his message couldn't have been more obvious.

And if all of us who witnessed the scene had carried signs that said WE CAN'T HELP YOU, *our* message couldn't have been clearer.

And what do you say to an eight year old kid who's lost his dog . . . especially when you know your words might stick in his mind the rest of his life?

This kind of call comes frequently.

"Squad 550, check a lost dog at 1700 West 26th."

Don and I answered that call knowing we had to be at our best. This was no easy assignment. This was a crisis. We knew from experience on this beat, the dog may have been the kid's only friend. We knew the boy's parents were probably drunks or junkies who didn't give a rip about him. We knew the lost dog no doubt represented Mom, Dad, Brother and Sister. We knew the boy had probably heard on TV you call a cop when you need a friend, so he mustered his courage and called. Well, he got two of the biggest ones in the neighborhood; together, Don and I make a 500 pound team.

The boy was crying when we arrived. "Hey, fella, what's the trouble?" Don asked, taking a handkerchief from his pocket to wipe the boy's tear stained face.

"Buster's gone," the boy sobbed. "You *will* find him for me, wontcha?"

How do we answer that question? Do we say, "Sure, sure we'll find him"?

What if we can't?

"Do you think he got run over?" the boy asked,

his voice shaking as he tried to control his fear.

And how do we answer *that* question? "Oh, no, Buster's all right"?

What if he isn't all right?

We know what we say at this point can make the boy a cop lover or a cop hater. We can be heroes or we can be villains. We can foster hope or create despair.

What message do we have for him? What magic words do we say? Do I speak of spring and baseball when it appears to the boy his spring will never come? Or even if it does, he doesn't care without his dog?

Police work is exciting all right, but Grief lags at the heels of every exciting moment. It tugs at the thoughts of every cop on the force. It whimpers at the door of every heart.

At the outset of my training, I had no idea how close a companion Grief would be. In both Bible School and Police Academy, I had been taught how to administer first aid in every kind of situation imaginable; but how do you put a splint on a broken heart?

And then there are the dying. What can a cop say to them? What are the words? What message should they convey?

I rode in one of the busiest squad cars in town and it was often my duty to keep life's beat going until medical help arrived. Sometimes I was able to do so. Often I was not.

On one occasion Don and I were driving slowly down an alley looking for a stolen car when we were called to check a P.I. near Main Beach at Lake Calhoun. Checking a P.I. means there's a car accident— that there are injuries.

There was no time to waste. We turned on the siren, the red lights and revved up the motor. "God, get this traffic out of the way," I prayed as we sped toward our destination. After several blocks of narrow escapes, we reached the scene of the accident. What we saw was sheer horror.

The street was a holocaust of shattered glass and jagged metal. Bodies lay in pools of blood. The injured moaned in pain. Others screamed in terror. Some staggered over debris in a state of shock while clutching wounds from which their life's blood poured.

Police almost always reach such an accident before the ambulance arrives and this was no exception. Don and I quickly administered what first aid we could and did our best to assure the desperate and the dying that further medical help was on the way. We covered the dead.

One young woman screamed uncontrollably as she pounded her fists on the ground beside her lifeless baby. The child had gone through the windshield at the point of impact, and the sight of the small mangled body made me cringe. This woman had brought that precious life into the world and now some drunken driver had taken it away.

I knelt beside her and put my arm around her shoulders. What could I say to her? I looked up into the face of my partner, searching for an answer. Don shook his head sadly as if to reply, "You're the preacher ... please say *something* that will help her."

But what words do I use? What message will ease her pain? "My God, my God," I cried silently —not in oath, but in prayer.

Restraining emotion, I spoke to her. I said some words, but what they were I don't remember. All I remember is that she kept screaming and pounding her fists on the ground.

Chapter II

The Concern

I was just getting ready to head for the ball park when I heard my mom call. "Allen Lee, would you come here a minute?"

Whenever she used both names like that, I knew there was an urgent matter before the house and that it concerned me. I hadn't done anything wrong to my knowledge, so I figured I was in for a session about life in general and what I was going to do with mine in specific. And I knew it would take longer than a minute.

"Son, you're twelve years old," Mom said when I entered the kitchen. "Your father and I feel it's time you start thinking about your life's goals."

"Yeah," I said. "I knew that's what you called me in here for."

Mother's green eyes brightened. "See there, Vernon?" she said to Dad. "Allen just knows things before people tell him. He'd make a good cop."

"He'd make a good preacher," Dad replied with a quiet firmness so typical of the manner in which he discussed all touchy topics with Mother. "God has marked him for the ministry."

"He's going to be tall and strong. He'd make a fine policeman," Mom said, "but if you insist on the clergy, he should be a priest."

"There's no way he can be a priest," Dad countered. "He's had girlfriends since he was in the third grade and I don't think he'll give them up for life."

As the debate continued the intensity of it increased to the point where I wanted to sneak out the back door but I didn't have the nerve. Nobody asked me what field I wanted to enter and I didn't quite dare suggest professional baseball though that idea had crossed my mind. One thing for sure, I didn't want to decide today.

This wasn't the first time—nor was it the last—my parents argued about what I should be. It was a constant thing with them and they never changed their minds—not ever. Always it was "Be a cop. Be a preacher. Be a priest."

Mom was full blooded Irish and a Catholic. Her family tree was so full of cops nobody could get by with a thing. Dad was a full blooded Swede and a Lutheran. His family tree had a minister on every branch. If the cops didn't get domestic matters straightened out, the preachers did.

I was an only child. How could I swing from two trees at once and make both Mom and Dad happy? It seemed at the time my parents were trying to run my life, but I know now the options they presented were part of a unique plan God had in store for me.

I became both—first a preacher, then a cop. When I finished my ministerial training at Bethany Fellowship in Minneapolis, I began preaching in various churches. My father was proud and happy. But all the while a growing conflict deep inside me kept me thinking about police work and what a challenge it would be. I prayed daily for God's guidance in the matter.

It seemed He wanted me to stay in my chosen profession. At least, that's what I thought when on a trip to New York, I encountered one of God's great ministers, David Wilkerson, who inaugurated the famed Teen Challenge in that city and subsequently wrote *The Cross and the Switchblade*.

Dave, though small in stature, is a giant for the Lord and miracles are an expected way of life for him. Though we'd never met prior to that encounter, Dave looked up at me with an intense gaze, pointed an index finger and said, "God told me you're supposed to work here."

My first inclination was to turn around to see if someone were standing behind me; but it was evident I was the object of his attention, and all I could do was gulp impulsively and blurt out, "Me?"

God's small giant nodded, and a week later my wife Gayle and I found ourselves living in New York— all our belongings packed in one suitcase!

My training session consisted of one sentence: "Go out on the street and trust the Lord." And so it was I became a member of the staff of Teen Challenge. Thus began a ministry that was to last four and a half years and one that was to prepare me for a life of service far beyond my human capacity to envision.

My desire to be a cop kept churning within, however, until one day I announced I would leave New York, return to Minneapolis and enter Police Academy.

"You're running from God," friends told me, but I was not to be disuaded even though I was plagued by guilt feelings over my decision. In attempts to expiate that guilt, I preached in churches seeking pastors and took my police tests concurrently. The day the city of Minneapolis hired me as a cop, a church in Wisconsin called me to be its resident pastor. I quickly said no to the latter and accepted the badge.

My mother was elated. No matter the occasion, she steered all conversation to one topic: her son, the cop. I was pleased she was happy. I was happy, too. I loved my job—so much so I tried to think of ways to work overtime. But guilt feelings kept me in a constant turmoil; I felt I had no business being a cop when I'd been trained for the ministry. Wasn't I, as my friends had said, actually running from God? Wasn't it wrong to follow my will, not His? And wasn't it almost blasphemous to be downright happy about it? I thought so even though I trusted the Lord with all the heart I could muster.

I know now my guilt feelings and doubts were not authored by my Heavenly Father. He permitted them to surface... perhaps to test my faith; but in my Christian walk with Him, I was not yet at the point where I could accept the fact He had given me the desires of my heart and that it was no sin to be happy about it. And I believe now, too, that were Jesus living on earth today, He would be found not so often in churches as on the streets and highways where sin sick souls travel in desperate need of a savior.

Since Friday and Saturday nights are always the "best" for action, I tried to work as many weekends as possible. And I preferred the beat from 7 p.m. to 3 a.m. since these are the peak crime hours. There are nearly twice as many crimes committed in these 8 hours as there are in the other 16.

One Saturday night, after only a few seconds on the street, all hell broke loose. Our first call took us to the fourth floor of an apartment building on 24th and Clinton where a man was threatening to kill his wife. Such calls are frequent and are often phonies. We take them seriously however; since were we to be careless, the result could be a couple of dead people.

This call was for real. There was no elevator; and since I was 8 years younger and 40 pounds lighter than Don, I led the sprint up the stairs. Just as I got to the apartment, a woman, her eyes wide with terror, rushed out and stopped me short. "He's drunk," she shrieked, clutching a faded robe about her body. "He's got a gun and he wants to kill a cop."

At that point Don joined me and I opened the door to face the adversary. A stream of profanities met my ears. The man staggered toward me and waved his gun precariously. "Take another damn step and I'll blow your brains out," he shouted in a demonic rage.

That he was temporarily insane was evident. Whether or not he meant what he said was not an issue to debate. In his confused frenzy, he could well have killed both of us whether he meant to or not.

Trying to reason with a drunk is like trying to read a newspaper in a high wind and I knew any attempt to do so would be futile. I had to somehow match his toughness and frighten him into submission. I don't know exactly what I said, but in essence I threatened to tear him a part unless he dropped the gun and came along peacefully. He kept waving the cold steel barrel at me, but I did my best to pretend I was ignoring it and looked him straight in the eye. To say I was not afraid would be an untruth; fear gripped me like a vice. The thought crossed my mind that I could die needlessly

... the victim of an irrational act ... a martyr for an empty bottle of booze. "Oh, God, don't let it happen," I prayed and there flashed into my thoughts the words "Ten thousand shall fall at thy side but it shall not come nigh thee ..."

I claimed His promise for myself that desperate moment and kept tough talking my way through the hazy stupor enveloping the mind of the man before me.

Reluctantly, he let the weapon fall, then kicked it toward us. Don handcuffed him while he bellowed, "I don't want to go nowhere."

His wife looked at him with tears in her eyes. He returned her gaze vacantly, unable to comprehend the sorrow written there.

"Come on," Don said as though talking to a child. "You're tired. You've had a hard day. We're going to take you to a nice soft bunk where you can get a good night's sleep." He came peacefully.

He'd sleep the jag off, then what? The problem was solved for tonight but not for tomorrow. I felt empty inside. Here was a human being created in God's image, acting in the manner of a crazed animal. We'd release him in the morning, but the liquid that enslaved him would keep him in its grip. Only God could set him free from that bondage. I wished I could tell his wife deliverance was on the way.

We no sooner left the jail than we were called to an OD, drug overdose. For four miles, red lights flashing and siren blaring, we sped to reach the victim, hoping Death would not reach her first.

She was on the floor ... just a young girl ... probably 16 or so. Scarcely breathing, she had started to turn blue. Hurriedly I turned her limp body over, grabbed her tongue, stuck my finger in her throat and cleared out some 15 pills. Don picked her up, threw her over my knee and slapped her with such force I thought my leg would break as well as the poor girl's back. But it did the trick. She began breathing normally and color returned to her face.

She'd wanted to die but we'd saved her life. Don radioed in to say she was OK; she wasn't, of course. She was simply alive, that's all. I'd been able to remove the deadly pills, but I couldn't reach into the depths of her heart and remove the loneliness and the hurt, the emptiness and the despair. Christ could do that for her and I wanted to tell her about Him, but we had to answer another call...fast!

This time a stick up was in progress at the Clark gas station on 22nd and Lyndale, just two blocks away. We pulled into the driveway within 10 seconds, just as the hold up vehicle was pulling out. Again with sirens and red lights, we took after the suspects. They went south on Lyndale, not stopping for intersections, cars or people. I was driving in city traffic at 90 miles per hour, trusting in the Power beyond myself to steady my hand at the wheel and clear the path so there would be no accidents along the way. Lyndale goes into Highway 94 which our stick up men took. I was relieved, for chances were good the highway patrol would help us. In a few moments, we saw their red lights a short distance behind us; and before I had a chance to think, red lights of another patrol were in front of us, forcing the hold up gang off the road. As a rule, highway cops don't get into gun fights or fist fights and this patrol waited for us to arrive. We pulled up behind and opened our doors. I grabbed the shot gun and pointed it at the car. Don used the PA system in our squad to order the men out, taking all the precautions so necessary to prevent dangerous altercations. Don was one good cop. He knew his business. "Throw your car keys out on the road," he ordered.

The driver obeyed.

"Now, one at a time, OUT. We want to see your hands behind your head."

There were four of them. As each man emerged from the car, he was ordered to kneel on the ground, cross his legs and keep his hands locked behind his head where we could see them at all times. At this point more squads arrived to assist us. We searched the suspects and booked them in the Hennepin County Jail. We learned they were addicts who couldn't find street drugs around. Often narcotics officers do such a good job at stopping the flow of drugs, junkies are forced to rob pharmacies for their goods. These young men had intended to do just that, but officers on a stake out at the drug store made them change their plans. They held up the gas station instead, hoping for enough money to pay for the now scarce commodities. A small plastic bag of heroin in the Twin Cities usually goes for $10, but during a drug panic the junkie is lucky to get it for $25.

My concern for drug addicts goes deep. I learned at Teen Challenge there's help for junkies who surrender to Jesus Christ and let Him be the Lord or Boss of their lives. These four young men needed to know that. I longed for the time, the opportunity to tell them ... but ... again, other calls preempted and I had to get back on the street. Again, another problem was taken care of ... just for a short time only.

I felt as though I'd been on duty all night, but a glance at my watch told me only four hours had passed. In that time, a man had tried to shoot us, we'd saved a young woman's life and we'd booked four hold up men after a long, high speed chase. That was a good night's work in any man's opinion.

We decided to take a short break and headed for Mr. Tina's Pizza House; but before we could appease our appetites, we were called to check a loud party on the 3600 block of Clinton. We get some ten loud party calls a week and they're no fun to take care of.

We pulled up in front of the house to find some 200 people mulling around, drinking, fighting, making love. The noise could be heard for miles. Don and I located the owner of the home and told him the party was over because too many neighbors were complaining. He was only 5'6" tall, but he was brave enough to tell us both to go to hell.

Don glared at him and spoke with thundering authority. "Listen, you midget turkey," he said. "You've got five minutes before we get the paddy wagon here and you'll be the first one in."

That convinced the party host. "OK, OK," he said and told the gang to shove off. They obliged.

Not all party calls were that easy. It bothered us.

A few months earlier, four blocks away, we'd issued another party the same kind of warning and were given quite some resistance. We told them to break up or go to jail—that was our rule: one warning, then jail. That group had not believed us. When we were called back we made our threat good and took ten other squads plus the paddy wagon with us. Six cars blocked the corners and the alley while the men in the other four squads went in. Don, the paddy wagon officers and I went to the front entrance; other officers went to the rear. Don beat on the door with his riot stick and it took some furious pounding to get above the sound of blaring music. Finally the door opened, then shut quickly in our faces. My partner was not about to be refused admittance. "Here's what you call crashing the party," he said as he took a few steps back, then lunged forward like a mighty steam roller.

The door flung open as if it'd been made of toothpicks. Needless to say, the "guests" were stunned. I walked over and turned the music off. "We're moving this party to the Hennepin County Jail," I announced and with that, officers swarmed in to usher the entire gang into the paddy wagon.

We then checked bedrooms, closets . . . every place we could think of. One bedroom produced a seventeen year old girl, so terrified she shook from head to toe. The bath tub produced two more. The last bedroom produced yet another two. I groped for the light switch when Don yelled, "All right, you two, break it up."

I hit the lights and saw what he had surmised: a couple engaged in the sex act. The boy was under five feet and weighed about 97 pounds. The girl was some six feet tall and weighed possibly 190 pounds. They were on the floor in the corner of the room, their faces flushed with embarrassment as they groped frantically for blankets with which to cover themselves. "You've got two minutes to get your clothes on," Don said. He always set a time limit and it was always short. It proved to be a workable philosophy since it got people moving in a hurry.

We left the room and waited outside the bedroom door. I began to feel sick from the stench of the filth and debris. Animals couldn't have stood living there. I wondered how these people stood it. The embarrased young couple came out and voluntarily headed for the paddy wagon. When all was said and done, we had arrested 35 people, seventeen of whom were under 18 years of age.

That was a typical loud party.

This one was too easy. It broke up with one threat. "There's something going on in there," I said. "We always get a lot of mouth, a lot of trouble when we break up a party."

We sat some ten minutes in utter silence to think this one over, then started tossing questions at each other. Why did the people leave so fast? Why did the little guy meet us on the front porch? How did he know we were coming? We never went into the house. What was in it we weren't supposed to see?

The average person would think things were all right once people left, but we were cops. We think differently. We're trained to be suspicious. Let's say Mr. Average is waiting for a bus when he sees a a man carrying a laundry bag. What does he think? He thinks the man is going to do his laundry. The cop thinks the guy could be out ripping people off. I've stopped numerous people carrying laundry bags because I'm suspicious. It would amaze Mr. Average to see how many bags contain jewelry, radios or even small TV sets just taken in a burglary.

So we were suspicious of this party because breaking it up was just too easy. We locked our car a few blocks down the street, came back to the house via the alley, climbed a tree and sat so that we could see through the window. Two heavy set cops up a tree struck me as amusing and I felt a bit silly to say the least. "We should've rented bird uniforms," I said to Don. "Then we could sit on that window sill and really get a good view."

"Yeah," he said wryly. "Nobody would suspect a thing if he saw a couple of 250 pound robins on a window sill."

Containing our laughter was difficult, but we had to and we had to be content with sitting in the tree and peering through the branches. After a few minutes we saw men coming in and going out of bedrooms. I saw things I would like to forget . . . sex acts I wouldn't dare reveal in print. We'd been suspicious for good reason. This was some kind of prostitution house. Had it been twenty years earlier, we could have kicked the door in and hauled everyone off to jail; but now, with lax court rulings, we didn't have that option.

We had a portage radio with us so we tried to contact the Morals Squad for advice; but failing to reach anyone, we returned to our squad and did the only thing we could do: make out a report. I was concerned to say the least. How I had wanted to get into that house! Those girls were no more than teen agers! The time would come when their moments of fleeting pleasure would turn into lifetimes of bitterness and remorse. They needed to know they could touch the hem of the Master's garment and depart free, fulfilled and forgiven.

We now had one hour left on our tour of duty and it went quickly. We took care of two gang fights and a car accident, then finished the night off by issuing a speeding ticket.

After work, Don and I sat in the squad room of the police station for awhile and sipped cokes. Though we didn't speak, each of us knew what the other was thinking. I got up, put my coke bottle away and walked back to my partner. "There was nothing more we could do," I said, placing my hand on his shoulder. "Let Morals take care of it. Better go home and get some shut eye."

I lived about twenty minutes from the station. All the way home I kept thinking about the girls in the prostitution house, the man who wanted to kill us, the girl who wanted to kill herself, the drug addicts involved in the stick up. I pulled into my garage and sat in my car for a time. I couldn't forget the people with whom we'd been involved that night. Some of the other cops appeared so cool and calm ... even cold. Nothing seemed to bother them but I was bothered. I knew the people we'd dealt with were people for whom Christ died. I knew He had a very personal plan for their lives. I knew He wanted to make them happy and fulfilled. But how in the world were they going to find that out? Each person had deep needs only Christ could meet. But not one of them hung around churches. Besides, not many churches had anything to do with such individuals. I thought of my commission as a Christian: "Go ye into all the world and preach the gospel." I was doing a pretty lousy job of it right here on the streets of my own city.

I finally got out of the car and went to bed. I didn't sleep. The thought kept plaguing me that in my work as a policeman, I was going around in circles ... following tire tracks in the snow.

I wanted to do something more than put people in jail.

Chapter III

The Decision

Something had to break. As things were, I couldn't continue being a cop since as the months went by, I found it increasingly difficult to justify my position on the force. Was I really helping anybody? Was I truly serving my Lord? Did He want me to remain in law enforcement? These questions continued to pound at me like a giant hammer.

It seemed many of the teachers in police academy wanted us to be content with getting a criminal off the streets by arrest. But that was only half the problem. The other half was reform. I'd heard from everyone the prison system was doing that part of the job—that it was helping people, not just punishing them. I'd heard it so much I started to believe it. It helped ease my conscience for a time and partially answer my question of whether or not I was accomplishing anything worthwhile. Sure I was. I was helping every citizen in Minneapolis. I was putting a concrete dent in the problem of making the streets a safer place. Every crook I arrested and put in jail made Minneapolis a better city in which to live.

At the end of each month, Don and I turned in a report of our activities, listing such accomplishments as making arrests, issuing traffic tags, locating stolen cars and so forth. One month I wanted to know how we rated with other officers so I checked the records. What I found surprised me. My partner and I had more credits on our list than had any other teams in three squads put together. The prisons were getting all kinds of people to reform from us.

But the longer I pondered the situation and looked at results, the more I realized the penal system wasn't reforming anyone. My eyes were opened to this fact after busting a young guy named Andy for car theft. The arrest was somewhat amusing in that it showed us Andy was no big time crook.

We were usually in an unmarked squad, but our car was being repaired so we rode in a marked squad on that hot, sticky July night. We were cruising down Lake Street, not thinking of busting anyone, but rather of getting some iced tea to cool off. A blue '67 Chevy was in front of us and I noted the driver kept looking at us in his rear view mirror. On one corner he was so nervous he forgot to check the traffic light and went right through on red. We didn't try to stop him since we knew many good drivers get so nervous when they see a police car, they'll make simple mistakes they wouldn't otherwise make. Sometimes our approach in a case like this is simply to watch for a time to see if there are further infractions. We made the wrong judgment in Andy's case, however. We should have stopped him right then, for two blocks later, his nervousness got the best of him. He looked in his mirror so often he missed another set of lights; then he missed the intersection, hit the light pole at about 25 miles per hour and knocked it flat.

We stopped to apprehend him and move the pole

so that it wouldn't block the street. Then we headed downtown to book our offender for a few traffic violations. On the way he talked our ears off and made a confession we hadn't asked for. He said he'd stolen the car about two hours before and was enjoying the luxury of just wheeling around. Then, as bad luck would have it, he made the mistake of turning on to Lake Street in front of two cops and went to pieces. "I got so uptight when I saw you two," he said, "I lost control of the wheel and knocked over that damn light pole."

Andy had stolen his first car, made his first attempt at being a cool crook and had failed miserably. The whole idea struck me as funny; and when we pulled up in front of the Hennepin County Jail, I was laughing so hard I could hardly pull him out of the car.

Our small time crook was sent to prison for 90 days and I was confident that would be the end of his short career in crime. It proved to be an invalid assumption on my part.

Two months later we were called to check on a prowler in a used car lot. Half a block before we arrived Don stopped the squad, I jumped out and went down the alley while he pulled up in front of the building. As we had anticipated, the prowler ran to the back of the lot, down the alley and straight into me. I held him against a car while I waited for Don; then we searched and handcuffed him and made our way to the Court House. "What's your name, buddy?" I asked as I began to write out a report.

"Come on, man, you know me," he said. "I was the one who knocked the traffic light down a coupla months ago."

"So you're Andy," I said with surprise. "How'd you get out so soon?"

"I was good," he said with a certain pride.

"Too bad it didn't last," Don said. "You're on your way back again, you know."

"That don't faze me," the kid said with a cocky sneer.

I was surprised by his attitude. Two months ago he'd been scared to death. Now he seemed hardened, calloused. What had happened to him? Even his appearance had changed, or so it seemed. At least, I hadn't recognized him. I wanted some answers. "Andy, did the prison officials try to help you?" I asked.

"Hell no," he said. "I just mopped a lot of floors."

"Why did you come right out and try to steal another car?" I questioned, attempting to find out what motivated this young man.

He looked me straight in the eye and gave me an answer I'll never forget. "The cons showed me how to steal better," he said.

I felt the blood rush to my cheeks in anger.

"Not only that," Andy continued, pleased by the interest we showed in his acquisition of knowledge, "I learned how to pick locks and sell drugs; and just before I got out, they were showing me how to pimp."

"How to *what*?" I said aghast.

"Look, man," he said, "there's good money in pimping. Hell, I could make so much money at it I could *buy* new cars if I wanted to."

Here was a 19 year old kid who before couldn't have pilfered a candy bar without getting caught, telling me he'd learned how to steal cars, pick locks, sell drugs and pimp. I was infuriated. I wanted to put the prison officials in jail. My mind raced as I tried to come up with some reason why I should remain a cop. My last argument was gone. I wasn't helping anyone. The people we put in the joint were coming back from crime schools, not from rehabilitation centers. I was seething with frustrated rage when Andy tugged at my arm. "Hey, officer Al, what's with you anyway?"

"I don't know," I replied. "I just don't know."

"Hey, man, buy me a pack of cigarettes, will ya?"

"Cigarettes," I said. "Did you learn to smoke in jail, too?"

"Yup," Andy said.

"What's bugging you?" Don asked, putting his hand on my shoulder as we stood at our lockers after the shift.

"You really want to know?" I asked.

"I have a hunch," my partner said, "but I'd like to hear it from you."

For an hour I unloaded everything that was on my mind. I told him how I had believed the police department and the prisons were doing their jobs until little by little I kept learning things that disturbed me. My last ray of hope was extinguished after finding out about Andy's training in jail. "Don, I've made up my mind to quit," I said. "I'm going to get back into some kind of ministry where I can really help people . . . something like the work I was doing in New York when I was involved with drug addicts and saw lives changed by Jesus Christ."

"Come on, Al," Don said quietly, "you can't give up. Where would this city be without its police force? We need good men like you."

"I've made up my mind, Don."

"Look, we can't change the world over night, but we're . . ."

"Save your breath," I interrupted. "I'm quitting."

"I hope you don't mean that," my partner said,

looking at the floor, "but somehow I have the feeling you do."

Gayle was up when I got home. She kissed my cheek, then drew back to look at me. "You're troubled," she said sympathetically.

"Yeah." I took her hands in mine and held them tight.

"Want to talk about it?"

I shook my head.

"Well, when you do, I've got an ear," she said quietly then added " ... and I'm behind you ... whatever you decide."

I looked at my wife with amazement. "How do you always just *know*?" I asked.

"Oh, I pray for insight," she replied matter-of-factly, as though it was the most natural thing in the world to expect answers to her prayers.

"I'm a lucky guy to have a girl like you," I said, "and I want you to know I appreciate you."

I couldn't sleep. I thought of New York and of all the young people I had worked with there. Some were much like Andy, others much worse. One I couldn't get out of my mind was a fellow named José Mena.

Every Tuesday night we had chapel services at Teen Challenge and I often conducted the meetings. The chapel was held in a long room with a door half way between the pulpit and the back wall. This was the room in which David Wilkerson preached to hundreds of drug addicts. This was the room in which Nicky Cruz sat listening to the messages that turned his life from one of hopelessness to one of glorious victory. If this room could talk, it would tell of miracles that would thrill the souls of every creature on earth.

On one particular Tuesday night, I was mid-way

through my message when in walked a young man who smelled so bad I ended my sermon right then and dismissed the meeting. The aromatic young guest came up to me and said he'd been a drug addict for seven years and was using $50 a day in heroin. He'd never been able to kick the habit but he wanted to desperately. I knew if he went cold turkey he'd become violently ill ... with something like the Hong Kong flu only 15 times worse. "What's your name?" I asked.

"José Mena."

"Do you believe in God?"

Without hesitation José replied that he did.

"All right, then kneel down and I'm going to pray for you. I'm going to ask God to heal your body so you won't have any withdrawal pains," I said.

José knelt, bowed his head and closed his eyes. I put one hand on him and asked God to perform a miracle in his body so he would have an easier time believing in His almighty love and power. When I finished, José stood to his feet, an air of quiet confidence about him. "Can I stay here at Teen Challenge?" he asked as though expecting an affirmative answer.

"It so happens we have one empty bed," I replied, "and I believe the Lord has reserved it for you."

I went back to my apartment that night wondering if God would really heal him ... if José would really be able to kick the habit without the accompanying pains of withdrawal. I went to bed and fell asleep. Some time later, I was awakened suddenly when my whole body jerked into a sitting position. The room was pitch black. The luminous dial on my clock said 3 a.m. A thought of José flashed through my mind then disappeared, and I was somewhat frightened. Had he been healed or was he in trouble?

Since my wife was in Minneapolis visiting with

her parents, I decided to get up and go to 96th and Broadway and talk with drug addicts. The middle of the night and early morning were always good times to find plenty of junkies in the streets. Besides, I knew I'd feel better to be busy. By mid-morning I headed for the Teen Challenge office with two young addicts: one who had been in the program and wanted to come back, and another who wanted to enter the program and get his life turned around.

I felt good about bringing the young volunteers in and headed for the kitchen where Dom, the cook, always had some goodies stashed away for me. While I ate and Dom and I talked, I noticed a lot of activity on the basketball court just outside the kitchen window. To my amazement there was José playing ball! I shoved my food aside and ran for the door.

"Where are you going so fast?" Dom asked.

"I've got to talk to that kid," I called back as I dashed to the court yard. José saw me coming and smiled from ear to ear.

"Feeling OK? You're not sick?" I asked apprehensively.

"I feel great," José answered with enthusiasm. "I've been healed!"

"Praise the Lord," I shouted. "He's a wonderful savior, isn't He?"

"Yeah, man," José affirmed. "He sure is to heal a rotten junkie like me."

"You're not a rotten junkie, José," I said. "You're a unique person to God. He has a special calling just for you."

"You're sure?" he asked, wide-eyed as though he hadn't expected any further benefits.

"As sure as I'm standing here."

My recollection of that experience was so clear I felt as though I had just relived it. Poor Andy. If only he could experience the power of Christ José experienced. But Andy was on his way back to prison for a second hitch. I thought of how angry I'd been when he spoke with pride about what he had learned there—so angry I'd told Don I was quitting the force.

Before I could begin to get some rest, Gayle called me to get up. "You've got a reporter coming to write a story about you, remember?" she said.

"Good heavens, I forgot all about it," I muttered as I dashed in to shower and shave.

A few days later the story was on the front cover of the Minneapolis morning paper. I was featured along with three other cops who had had ministerial training.

Following that, thoughts of quitting the police department became stronger and stronger. Should I or shouldn't I? I was torn with indecision until one day I called out to God and demanded an answer. Then I sat completely still until slowly and very distinctly God spoke. "Go back to Teen Challenge."

The words were so clear there was no mistaking them.

At that moment the phone rang. It was Frank Reynolds, the director of Teen Challenge in Rehrersburg, Pennsylvania. Rehrersburg is the place to which all the East Coast centers send people for advanced Bible training.

"Al, I'm in Minneapolis at North Central Bible School and your news article is on the bulletin board," Frank said. "Would you possibly consider leaving The Cities and coming to Rehrersburg to head up our drug education ministry? We're getting into hundreds of schools . . ."

Without hesitation I said yes, knowing God had just that instant given me a direct answer to my prayer.

I quit my police job, took care of my bills and moved my family to Rehrersburg, a little town of

200 people halfway between Lebanon and Reading, Pennsylvania. But as soon as we had unloaded the truck, I began to miss my job. Everyone on the force had told me I'd be back. "Police work gets in your blood," they'd said.

They were right. As the weeks went by, I felt more and more of a loneliness for the beat. At the same time, however, being involved with Teen Challenge again was great. I was working with people from the streets and I loved it.

When I'd been in Rehrersburg for six months, my boss left to be director for the Cleveland Center and I was put in charge of both drug education and fund raising. By the end of the year I wanted to get back into police work so badly I felt I was literally going mad. But I was in a real fix now. I had left the force because I wasn't helping anyone. Now I was helping hundreds of kids but I wanted out. What in the world was going on in my head? Did I know my own mind or didn't I? I began to doubt my sanity.

A few days later Mother called saying Dad had had a heart attack and that his condition was critical. I left for Minneapolis immediately, asking God to keep my dad alive at least until I could see him once more and to help me know my future.

Before the plane landed, He spoke to me by instilling certain thoughts in my mind: 1. my dad would be all right; 2. I was to get back on the force because there were things I had to learn about God's plan for law officers; 3. my work in Rehrersburg had not been a mistake, rather it had given me necessary training which would be of value to me later; and 4. there were many areas of ministry I would see coming out of police work.

Now all I had to do was to get myself hired again.

I knew that wouldn't be easy.

Chapter IV

The Return

While God often grants instant answers to prayers, as He has so many times in my life, it sometimes takes awhile for all the details to fall into place; and I was to find that out in this situation.

The waiting period will be what the Christian makes it to be. He can worry and fret and wonder if God is really working on his case, so to speak, and take it out of His hands now and then by trying to handle the problem himself; or he can, if he truly believes God knows what He's about, simply wait patiently, trusting all is well and even eagerly anticipating the eventual outcome which he knows will be far better than he could envision. There's a lot of peace in following the latter course! And joy!

It takes discipline to get to that point in the walk of faith where one is *able* to do so! But it's at *that* point the Christian can actually rejoice in the "seeming" obstacles along the way—in the "seemingly" adverse conditions that arise, for he just *knows* all things are working together for his good.

I hate to see the faint hearted give up when hard conditions come. Often they'll say, "I prayed for what I knew was in accordance with His will and just look what happened!"

The one who thinks that way and subsequently acts upon that thinking, can delay—even prevent—from coming, the good God has in store for him.

Getting rehired was not easy and the approach I took in facing the difficulty lay somewhere between the two courses just related. It was Gayle who kept reminding me, through the delays, that all things were actually working for my good.

I was to find out, however, the assurance I'd been given that Dad would be all right was one of those immediate answers to prayers. When I drove to the hospital in Crosby, the town in Minnesota where my folks had retired, I found Dad sitting up in bed looking great. There was color in his face, a sparkle in his eye and still the zest for life that had always been such an inspiration to me.

He was somewhat dismayed to hear I was quitting Teen Challenge and that didn't surprise me. After all, he'd been the one who, throughout my childhood, had said, "Be a preacher."

"Are you sure it's the right thing to do, Son? he asked looking me straight in the eye with that intense gaze of his. "I mean, of *course* your mother and I would like to have you back in Minneapolis where'd you be closer to us, but I always felt you were marked for the ministry."

"God has spoken to my heart about it, Dad," I replied.

Not Dad's to question his creator. "Oh, well then, of course you must follow where He leads you," he said. And I did.

I took my first step. I spoke to Chief of Police, Gordon Johnson, who told me he wanted me back on the force. "This is going to be simpler than I anticipated," I thought.

Gordon turned me over to his aide to work out

the details and I was told by him to come to work
in two weeks. Overjoyed, I ran to the nearest
phone, called Teen Challenge in Rehrersburg and
resigned. Reverend Reynolds was understanding, as
always, and gave me his blessing. He wasn't one
to presume upon God either and felt since it had
been His guidance that led to my decision, he
wouldn't try to talk me out of it though he was sorry
to see me go he said.

I returned to Pennsylvania and Gayle and I
readied ourselves for the move, both excited about
the challenges that lay ahead in Minneapolis. But
my spirits took a nosedive when I got a call from
the chief's aide. "We're sorry, Al, but the council
just put a freeze on all city jobs and I can't hire
you."

Now what? I had quit my job at the center. No
course but to unquit it and get myself hired again.
To put it mildly, I was getting a bit spooky about
the whole business. Surely my supervisor would think
me a spineless character who swayed whichever way
the wind blew. Had I interpreted God's lead correctly? Or was I putting thoughts into my own head?
Or had God, perhaps, changed His mind?

"Hardly," Gayle assured me. "He won't tell you
one thing one day and the opposite the next."

"I know you're right," I said, "but maybe I'm
getting the messages all mixed up."

"Don't presume upon the 'maybe's' when you deal
with the Lord," Gayle continued. "He told you He
wanted you back on the police force and He'll work
it out. Don't worry about it."

"Can't help it," I replied.

"Would you call God a liar?" my wife asked
bluntly.

"Of course not," I said, somewhat shocked she'd
ask such a thing.

"Well, that's what you're doing when you worry about it," she said. "You're doubting what He told you is true. And if it isn't true it's a lie."

Those were pretty harsh thoughts, but I pondered them awhile and realized they were right on. I decided then and there I would doubt no more; rather that I would move along the obvious, logical path until things opened up in Minneapolis. I went back to my supervisor, Frank Reynolds, and explained the situation, asking him to rehire me and let me stay for as long as it took for things to work out with the police force. By all human understanding he should have said, "You can't be serious; there's no way I'd permit that," but Frank was a devoted Christian. He didn't follow the natural line of reasoning. He did the unnatural thing. He rehired me, knowing I wouldn't be around very long.

As time went on, I got a case of the doubts again. I'd had no word from the chief's aide so I decided to call him. "Things are still bad here, Al," he said. The President of the Police Officers Federation is working on it, but the freeze on jobs looks as if it's here to stay for quite awhile. Don't get your hopes up too high."

Might as well tell fish not to swim. How could I help getting my hopes up? When I got home that night I related to Gayle what the aide had told me. "The President of the Federation is working on it," I said.

"That means God is working on it," she added.

Who was I to doubt that statement? "If God be for us, who can be against us?" I added, suddenly uplifted by having recalled that scripture verse. "Now why didn't I think of that before?"

"I think because you needed to remember it just now," Gayle said softly.

And so I went about my work, reminding myself

to be patient because God was about the business of working things out and there was nothing I needed to do to prompt Him along. As a result, I wasn't surprised when two weeks later I received the call telling me what we'd expected to hear. The city council had approved my assignment. They'd been convinced by the Federation that hiring me would save them money in that they wouldn't have to pay for training a new man. The freeze on jobs was going off and I was going on! Praise the Lord! God had overruled the city council! I was overjoyed as was Gayle. We began the task of packing.

I wanted to go back to my old squad car area, but I was assigned to the third precinct which is, for the most part, a fairly quiet district in South Minneapolis. I confess I didn't like that beat the first night back. It was too easy to my way of thinking. I preferred my old area where I was busy all the time with heavy stuff. Once in awhile, however, things got busy in this quiet neighborhood.

As happened my second day back when I saw a car roaring down the street at dusk, doing 60 miles an hour in a 30 mile zone past a park full of children. It took me about 10 blocks to catch the speeder, but I caught him.

Using my flash light, I checked the inside of the car to make certain no one was lying on the floor with a gun. That happens sometimes, and the precaution is a wise one to take. This back seat was empty.

"Good evening, Sir. Could I see your driver's license please?" I asked.

He handed it to me reluctantly and asked why he'd been stopped. Surely he must've known. I looked at him for a moment and thought how much I'd like to grab him by the neck and say, "Look, stupid, you just sped by a park full of kids. You could have killed one or two without even knowing it.''

But I didn't. Instead, I responded with a question. ''Why do *you* think you were stopped?'' I asked.

He thought for a time then admitted perhaps he was going a little too fast.

''A *little* too fast?'' I admonished. ''You were going 30 miles an hour over the limit!''

''You sure, Officer?''

I assured him I was certain. ''Look, what would you have done if those children had run into the street after a ball? That happens all the time, and they don't always look for cars.''

The man was silent.

I answered the question for him. ''You wouldn't have been able to stop. You might have killed one of those kids. My partner and I would then have had to tell his parents some reckless idiot had just run over their child.''

''Well, it didn't happen,'' the man said. ''Give me a break, will you?''

''I'll give you a break,'' I assured him. ''I'll give you a tag so you won't forget this conversation.''

''But ...''

''And let me say I'd hate to be in your shoes if I ever catch you speeding in a zone like this again,'' I said.

I was angry. I'd been in the position of having to tell parents about the death of a child and I confess it's the most difficult task any officer can have. It's terrible. There aren't words to describe it. I had two small children of my own and I was thinking of buying a home in the South Minneapolis area. I cared, as I knew all parents cared, about making the streets safe; and I have no sympathy for the speeder. The very fact this man had made me follow him for ten blocks indicated there was no room for leniency in dealing with him.

I was glad, however, I hadn't had to take him on in a lengthy high speed chase since such assignments always make me uptight. Obviously the "chasee" doesn't want to stop and obviously the "chaser" is in danger and can endanger the lives of others. I'd had a bad taste or two from having been involved in such speed chases and I didn't like them even though I'd been well trained for that type of assignment.

I'd been given courses in speed driving while in Police Academy; those were downright fun. The real thing was not. Our training consisted of cops chasing "robbers" around the Metropolitan Stadium where the Minnesota Vikings and Twins play. Our instructors put us in all sorts of problem situations. One in particular was chasing the getaway car after a supposed bank robbery. The mock robbers drove battered unmarked cars while the rest of us drove the older, marked police cars. We had the whole bit— red lights, sirens and all. We chased each other around the stadium all day learning different safe ways of stopping crooks. We took our training seriously and obviously some passers by did, too.

One man, who had witnessed police officers getting beaten up bodily, was so concerned he called the Bloomington police station and two of their men sped out on the double. How relieved they were to find out we were merely in training!

At the end of the session, our instructor made it clear that some of us had better not make the mistakes we'd made that day because we wouldn't be going home alive if we did.

I wasn't out on the beat as a "real" cop for long when I had the opportunity to use my training at that stadium. My partner and I were on 38th and

Lyndale when we saw a white Ford go through a traffic light. We put on our red light, beeped the horn and even called to the driver over our loud speaker. She gave us no indication she intended to stop and kept that Ford moving as if her life depended on getting somewhere in a hurry. I was driving the squad and all I can remember is that Don called our street location to the radio dispatcher. I was doing 80 on the city streets, dodging in and out of traffic, turning corners almost on two wheels and just barely missing cars and people.

"Doesn't that take nerve?" people ask. "Isn't it frightening?"

Yes, it takes guts. No, it's not unusual to feel the muscles tighten and to be scared to death. But one has to keep his cool . . . and pray.

All of a sudden the white Ford went out of control and ran into a brick wall. Within ten seconds other squads were there . . . they'd been trying to block off the streets in an attempt to help us.

Not knowing what the situation was, Don and I approached the car slowly, shotguns in hand. What we saw was horrifying. Two young girls, both unconscious, lay sprawled over the front seat midst broken glass and torn metal. When I opened the door, the driver fell into my arms. She was bleeding badly, but she was alive and her pulse was strong. There were five areas of her body to which I had to apply pressure in order to stop the bleeding. Obviously her condition was serious, and she'd most certainly have bled to death had we not been able to administer emergency first aid.

I estimated the ages of both to be seventeen. The passenger had been hit on the head and when she came to, she became hysterical at seeing her friend wrapped in bloody bandages. We sent the injured girl to the Hennepin County Hospital by ambulance and took her partner to our squad while we waited for the tow truck to haul away the accident vehicle.

"Why didn't you stop?" I asked her when she'd calmed down somewhat.

She sat silently for a time, then said, "Neither one of us has a driver's license."

"Whose car was it?"

"My dad's," came the reply.

"You mean your father let you take the car without a license?" I asked.

"He didn't know we took it," she confessed. "We'd done it before and never got stopped by police. We just didn't know what to do when we saw your red lights."

"You know now," I said. "Too bad you had to learn the hard way."

"Yeah," she said, wiping the tears from her face with a ragged sleeve. "We sure were dumb. I'm scared what dad'll say."

We took the girl to the hospital for a check to see if there were head injuries and called her parents.

As soon as they arrived to get their daughter, we received a report of trouble at a pizza place on Lake Street. Several young men were raising a ruckus—breaking chairs and glasses and throwing food at each other. We barged in midst laughter and dodged a few pizzas before we got the group settled down. Don called for help just in case we couldn't handle the crowd—there were 8 of them. Then we both walked over to them, our hands on our night sticks. As we stood before them, their noise level diminished considerably. They sat looking at us, wondering what we would do.

"Do you have any idea why we're here?" I asked.

No one answered.

"We're here to take an offering to cover damages," I said; and with that, Don took off his hat and put it on the table. One fellow got up and started for the door. Don grabbed him with one hand and lifted him off the floor. "Hey, you forgot to give a donation," he said.

The young man quickly put a $5 bill into the hat. No one else followed.

"You've got 30 seconds to come up with fifty bucks or you're all going to jail for property damage," I said and I meant it.

"You think you can arrest all eight of us?" one big fellow asked with a sneer.

We took our sticks out of their holders. "Yes," we said in unison. "But we may have to take you to jail via the county hospital first," I added.

I didn't want to take on all eight and neither did Don. Obviously we both hoped our help would hurry in getting there. Within seconds, our hopes materialized. Four police officers strode through the door and thirty seconds later, Don's hat was full of money. The manager counted out $48 and said that would be sufficient.

We told the crowd to get out fast, cut the clowning for good and not to come back. They obliged sheepishly and willingly. As we watched them drive away Don said, "Thank your lucky stars we don't have to give them a chase. Looks like those cars are souped up for fast getaways."

"For sure," I agreed. "Best we keep our eyes open for *that* gang."

My first high speed chase in the new district lasted five blocks and I lost the "chasee." No lives were endangered but even so, with the memory of the two girls still fresh in my mind, I felt uneasy. Quite a few policemen are hurt or killed each year because of such chases and I hated them. I liked to go home in one piece after work.

The action started when a motorcycle zoomed from an alley at night with no lights on, barely missed cars stopped at an intersection and careened into an alley. I turned to follow him. "Hit him, hit him!" my team mate yelled.

"If I do, I'll kill him!" I shouted. I was just inches from the rear end of his cycle and I knew impact at such speed would be lethal. My decision was to take middle ground. I rammed him five or six times as gently as I could, figuring he'd have to do one of two things: either stop for fear of his life, or go faster for fear of getting caught. He opted for the latter. Before we knew it, he turned in between two houses and we found ourselves stuck in the mud when we tried to follow. The culprit then zoomed through the back yard, down a hill and over a curb. It took me some 90 seconds to get free and by that time the phantom had disappeared. We looked all over South Minneapolis but couldn't find him. Lucky for him we couldn't. And lucky, too, that he picked totally at random, a back yard with no fence and no clothes lines.

In many ways I was starting to like the quieter way of police work I found in South Minneapolis. During my first stint on the force I was in such a busy area I never had time to think in between calls and often my head would spin. Often we arrested so many people that by the time we got to court, we couldn't remember what they'd done. For example, there were nights Don and I arrested up to 100 people and that's an incredible number.

Heavy crime wasn't the only problem in that busy district. People drove their cars like crazy and Lake Street was often a drag strip. Every year when the weather got warmer, we could hear the engines roar and the tires squeal. But we were so busy most of the time we couldn't do much in the way of enforcing traffic laws. In between calls we'd write tickets mostly for drag racing. It wasn't just the city kids who raced on Lake Street. Kids came from all over the suburbs to race there. I patched up so many cuts and broken heads I often felt as though I were working part time at general hospital.

Drag racing may seem harmless to many, but serious accidents often result and there's no course but to be tough with the clowns who consider such idiocy fun.

One kid I'll never forget was a runt from 25 miles south of downtown Minneapolis. He figured his car was the hottest thing on wheels. To prove his point he started challenging everybody in the business.

We had certain places we'd hide in order to catch some of these dragsters; and once while in our favorite spot, we saw a green streak zoom past us, another car alongside. We always try to catch both cars if we can, but this time it was impossible. We did manage to get the green car, however. The driver stood barely 5 feet tall and was as crusty as they come. While I checked his driver's license, Don found three things to which the car was in violation of: the most significant was that the rear of the vehicle was 38 inches above the ground. The limit's 20.

"What are you doing on Lake Street?" I asked.

"I just like to drag my car," he said as if I were stupid to ask.

His attitude got to me. I grabbed his shoulder and held him firmly. "Are you listening or aren't you?" I said, "because if you aren't we'll take you to a quiet cell where you can hear better."

"I hear ya, I hear ya," the kid said.

We told him to take his hot car out of Minneapolis and drag it in the suburbs. To that he replied he couldn't. We knew the reason, of course. There were fewer crimes in those areas, hence more police officers were free to watch for traffic offenders.

I released my grip and the hot rodder swaggered back to his car. Before he left I told him if I ever saw him drag racing in Minneapolis again, I'd arrest him. "What's more," I added, "I'll tow your car away and give you so many traffic tags you can use them for wallpaper."

Many people don't know a person can be arrested and jailed instead of being given a traffic tag or ticket. Most of the time, however, a ticket is issued and the offender can either pay it or opt to fight it in court.

Either our runt didn't take us seriously or else he was a total dimwit. The next day we saw him dragging Lake Street again. Needless to say, we kept our promise. We took him to jail, had his car towed in and gave him approximately 20 different tickets.

We couldn't waste time being lenient with such offenders. The reason is obvious. Their cars are unsafe and their carelessness injures and kills many people each year.

Somehow word of what we'd done to the cocky kid got around. Lake Street stopped being a drag strip at Hiawatha Avenue which was not part of my district.

While I grew to like the slower pace in my new district, there were days I longed for that busy beat. Sundays were by far the most difficult days for me in South Minneapolis. Not because they were slow. I expected that. But I was bothered by the number of people not in church. I've found that most of those who get in trouble with the law are not church goers.

My theory, of course, is that the principles taught in Sunday School rooms and from behind pulpits make an impression on people. They take the messages to heart and try to live as law abiding citizens.

I think I was upset most by seeing droves of children playing in the streets on Sunday mornings. I had always felt it important to "train up a child in the way he should go . . ."

If parents weren't taking their children to church or sending them, who would do it?

I was concerned. So much so I began to feel God was trying to tell me something . . . something related to what he had revealed to me on the plane months earlier.

Chapter V

The Realization

My concern about the kids not being in church on Sundays was so intense, I was just plain uptight; and for the life of me, I couldn't figure out why. Oh, there was the obvious reason ... I was a Christian. I knew the love and the peace they could acquire for adulthood by being schooled in God's ways as children. I knew what they were missing out on. But there was more to it than that. Much more. Something I couldn't quite put my finger on and that bugged me. So there I was going around in circles again. And that bugged me, too.

But I figured I was on the right track even though work in the quiet area wasn't totally satisfying. I *was* back on the force and God had worked that out for me. That was one of the revelations He'd given me on the plane some months earlier. A second was that Dad would be all right and now he was. I felt certain the other would materialize in time: many avenues of ministry would evolve from police work. But I was anxious to know when those avenues would open up and how I was going to fit in. Perhaps *impatient* is the word. I kept praying for guidance and along with that, kept wondering why I wasn't completely happy to be back where I'd wanted to be. And then, too, there were still those occasions when the unrest in my soul brought the recurring doubt: was I *really* where God wanted me to be?

I guess to put my dilemma into words, I wanted to know what I was going to be when I grew up and I was almost 30 years old.

"The Sunday Syndrome," as I called it, got to be a habit with me. It was as if I told myself every week, "Today's the day I'll be bugged about kids in the streets when they should be in Sunday school."

Then I'd see them later and the disturbance would well within to the point where I wanted to load them all in a paddy wagon and haul them off to the nearest place of worship. In my mind I could look years ahead and see myself hauling them off to jails for the whole variety of crimes ensuing from lives of bored inactivity, rebellion and parental neglect. But who was I to even think of forcing a matter which should be a voluntary action on the part of the parents? Of course it couldn't be done by force, but many were the times I wished it were possible.

One particular Sunday morning, though, I wasn't bugged. Cruising around the parks and streets, I found myself thinking of other things, no victim of the syndrome. When I realized I'd completely spaced it out, I wondered why and thought perhaps God was trying to tell me something. It was as if my mind, quiet for once, was open so that He could get through to me. My partner on that morning, out of a clear blue sky, said something which triggered a whole series of questions and answers for me. He simply asked, "Al, how many people go to church these days?"

I hadn't even thought of that. What was the answer? How many people *do* go to church? And of those who go, how many are serious about it? I confessed I had no idea how to answer his question but determined then and there I'd do some research on the subject. I dug into statistics and, pooling all the information I was able to unearth, came up with quite a shocking answer. At least it was shocking to me. Only about 50% of the people in the United States attend church. Only from 18 to 20% attend any sort of mid-week service. If one can assume that the group attending the mid-week service is the group serious about living by the principles of Christianity, then the percentage upon whom church has an influence is very small to say the least.

The 50% who did not attend services of any kind comprised the group, I believed, from which we derived most of our "business" on the police force. I didn't have any exact way to prove that theory, but I did some research directly with the people I arrested and came up with statistics I believe to be indicative of the situation across the country. Of every person I asked some basic questions, taking care not to infringe on personal rights or court decisions. The number of those having any kind of church life was small, practically infinitesimal . . . and almost none had any kind of active church involvement.

From the standpoint of the gospel and what I felt its message to be, I was concerned. I wanted to reach those unchurched people. Jesus commissioned all Christians to preach the gospel and to make disciples. From the standpoint of police work, I was not sure I should be concerned at all. I had a job to do and it involved that group which was breaking the law. There wasn't time on the job to do more. No one on the force seemed to care about getting to those people except me and I couldn't get them out of my mind. But how could I obey the words of Christ and be a policeman at the same time? There seemed to be no way. Yet He had most certainly led me into law enforcement. And even though police work brought me more satisfaction than any other work I'd done, something was wrong. Something was missing and I knew it.

There were, however, those worthwhile experiences. Finding lost children was one. Seeing happy parents was well worth whatever trouble it took to locate their youngsters. There were times it brought a lump to my throat and tears to my eyes. Even the toughest of cops showed emotion, or tried to hold it back, on those occasions. Even big tough Don shed a few tears of joy now and then. And, of course, the many times we saved lives brought deep satisfaction that only we as policemen could know . . . a sort of intangible fringe benefit of the job . . . unnoticed by the public in general and often unappreciated, even by the ones whose lives we saved. Thank you's were few and far between.

On the other side of the coin, there were lives we saved that to all human reasoning didn't seem worth saving. But who were we to judge? We could not help wondering though. As was the case, or so it seemed, on one occasion when my partner and I were called to a stabbing one night over on 25th Street in South Minneapolis.

She lay on the floor of her living room in pools of blood which spurted and poured from every part of her multilated body. Curious neighbors with morbid interest stood by to witness our hurried attempts to stop the bleeding from over 40 stab wounds inflicted by some unknown assailant who obviously had been mad with the desire to kill. Not one person had tried to help her though the woman had screamed for help. One, thank heaven, had had the presence of mind and the concern to call the police; and as a result of that call, we were able to get there in time to save the victim's life. It maddened and frustrated me to have to force the people to stand back to give us room to administer aid and to give the woman air.

She reeked of alcohol—anesthetized to the point she didn't feel the pain which would have been excruciating. She'd be feeling it when she sobered up, but now she simply moaned—uncomfortable, drunk, oblivious to the life saving moves being made in her behalf.

I worked feverishly . . . the only thought racing through my mind being "We must save this woman's life." And we did it.

Afterwards, while the men with the stretchers hauled her away in an ambulance, I came to, so to speak, and felt like retching from the odor of blood and the suffocating fumes of alcohol. I reeled, then regaining my balance, made my way hurriedly to the squad car, Don close behind, aware I was having a problem.

We went to a diner for a pick-me-up which meant soda pop for me and coffee for Don. We gulped compulsively and tried to collect our wits and our composures. I couldn't speak. Didn't want to. But Don broke the silence. "Talk to me, will ya?" he asked. "You're too darned quiet. Scares me. Are you freaking out or what?"

I stared at him. "It isn't the first mess we've patched up," he continued. "So a guy never gets used to it . . . so it helps to rap a little . . . get it outta your system . . . "

"I feel lousy," I said.

"We pulled her through. Doesn't that make you feel something?"

"So we pulled her through," I said with uncertain sarcasm. "Was it worth it? She lives like a pig. She's a drunk and a whore. She's raising a bunch of kids to be crooks. She won't change. What's the use?"

"Your religion going sour? Giving up on saving lost souls or what?"

Don's question wasn't cynical. It was an earnest request for an answer. For a brief moment I was ashamed of the implied testimony I'd given by my discouragement. Of *course* saving the woman's life had been worth our efforts. What's the use? I couldn't answer that but I knew the God in charge of the universe could. Surely He had a plan for her life even though it wasn't given me to know what it was. Had it been His will to permit the woman to die, no effort on my part or on Don's could have saved her life.

When I explained those thoughts to Don who seemed to understand, I felt led, once again, into inviting him to accept Christ in a personal act of contrition and faith. "You know, Don," I said, "He wants to be the Lord of your life, too."

Don shifted in his seat and stared into the cup which he held in both hands, tipping it this way and that to see how close he could get the coffee to the rim without spilling it.

"You agree with that?" I said finally.

"Yeah, sure, I agree," he said quietly, then gulped the rest of his coffee. "But today's not the time and this isn't the place. Let's split."

"Don, I think . . . "

"Al, *I* think," he interrupted, "that we oughta save the lives and let God save the souls."

He had a point. I let the matter drop. We went back to work.

Somehow I felt better. Don had unknowingly reminded me God was handling His affairs, and my job was to handle mine.

For some reason I turned the black and white into an alley. It was night. The frosty orange light of a full moon made artistic silhouettes of the things daylight revealed as back street clutter. It was then the awful sound of something non-human met my ears and I stopped the squad to listen. "Someone or some thing is in pain," I whispered to Don, "but I don't hear it now."

"Well, I'll be doggoned," he said as he spied the source of the noise. "Now *there's* something you gotta see to believe." He pointed to a clothesline in the yard to our left. An elongated figure hung from the wire, jerking, twisting, spinning.

"What in the world *is* it?" I asked.

"It's a dog . . . a young collie. He's hanging by his collar to that line."

I was incensed. "It takes a savage to do something like that."

"World's full of 'em," Don said. We scaled the fence and dashed to the animal victim.

Don held the now limp creature up to relieve the pressure on its neck while I unhooked the collar chain. Somehow our crude attempts at resuscitation worked and the animal started breathing again.

"Come on, Boy. That's a good dog. Now keep it up. Nice and steady, Boy."

"How'd you get in that predicament, Fella?"

As we spoke to the collie, he began to wag his tail. By this time the family had come out to see what was going on. The dog licked our faces, then jumped up to greet everyone with enthusiasm, as though he wanted to tell the whole story. He ran back to Don and me, stood in front of us and wagged his tail excitedly. We knew it was his way of saying thanks. When we explained what had happened, the puzzled father just scratched his head. "How in blazes did he get himself hooked up there?" he asked.

"Do you suppose someone did it deliberately?" the wife added.

Don surveyed the scene. He was good at solving mysteries. "More likely he jumped up on that picnic table there," he said, "then jumped up maybe to catch something buzzing around in the light. Came down on the line and got himself hooked."

"Yeah, he'll jump up after moths and bugs," the small boy said as he grabbed each of us by a leg and squeezed. "Thanks, Mr. Policeman and Mr. Cop. You saved Corky's life."

"Yes, thank you, Officers," the parents said.

"Corky's already thanked us," Don replied, patting the collie who was licking his hand and slapping his tail against my leg. He turned to the dog. "And *you* watch out for clothes lines from now on, understand?" The animal barked as if to say he did and we left the place feeling good about what we'd been able to accomplish.

On the way home that night, I thought about the appreciation we'd received from the collie and how both Don and I had been able to communicate with him. And I thought, too, of the scripture, "His eye is on the sparrow." The Lord knew Corky needed us that moment and sent me intuitively turning into that alley where we found him. It was a good feeling to know through direct guidance, He'd been leading us to the place He wanted us to be. One thing I felt certain of . . . I was no longer to question the value of the lives we saved. All were important to Him.

I soon had another opportunity to save a life. My

partner at that time was going to school which meant he would be late for work, so for an hour and a half I worked alone. I no sooner hit the street than one of the detectives radioed in that he'd come across a P.I., personal injury accident. "It's a bad one," he said, "and I don't have a first aid kit."

Seventy seconds later I was on the scene. A small red Ford was smashed against a tree . . . the driver had been thrown some 30 feet from the car. "Dear God," I asked instinctively, "why must Your people drive so carelessly? And why, oh why, don't they wear their seat belts?"

The night was cold . . . one of the coldest I could remember working . . . 24 below zero. And there was a brisk north wind that made it seem even colder. Here again the woman was bleeding from so many parts of her body, I hardly knew where to begin. I worked fast, kneeling on the ground beside her and bandaging the wounds to stop the onrush of blood. First the neck, the forehead . . . the top of her head . . . the arms. When I finished, the poor woman looked like a mummy, but she was alive. The ambulance arrived and I left. My knee was frozen and it hurt so bad I could scarcely walk. It gave me trouble for some time, but that didn't matter. I had saved a life. She'd have bled to death had I not gotten there as fast as I did. A person can bleed to death in a very short time. There's not a second to waste, for without the blood, there can be no life. Just as there can be no salvation without the blood . . .

Saving lives . . . night after night. "We'll save the lives, let the Lord save the souls," kept running through my mind as I went home early that morning. Yes, but it takes a human agent to save those lives. Didn't God use human agents to lead souls to Him?

Of course He did. But when was I going to have the opportunity to do just that on the police force? Or was I?

I couldn't answer the question.

Chapter VI

The Rescue

The night we rescued the unfortunate Henry Logan was memorable in that the reign of terror he'd been a voluntary victim of for so long came to an end as the result of a trumped up charge no one except his accuser understood. It was the night he had the book thrown at him . . . and even *he* admitted that was better than what he'd been used to.

We were to be prepared for the strange explanation to an even stranger set of circumstances by what happened earlier when we stopped a woman we should have let go . . . at least for one more block.

When she sped by us on 38th Street, 20 miles over the limit, we set out after her. A fleeting glance prompted the thought she didn't look like the lawbreaking type but the first impression proved invalid. She increased her speed and kept on going as if she were headed for a garage sale.

"Flaky female," Don muttered. "Wonder what *her* story is."

Thirty-seven-36-35-34—we whizzed by the street signs trying to catch her until 26th and Chicago where we finally got the job done. Don looked my way to see if I'd object to sitting this one out. "She's all yours," I said. "Lay a ticket on her."

"I'll do better than that. That broad darn near caused a coupla accidents."

He jumped from the squad and strode angrily to the woman who had rolled her window partially down to accommodate him. Don began to write out a ticket. I watched as the woman handed him her license. She fidgeted nervously and it appeared her conversation was quite animated. Suddenly Don stopped writing, looked inside the car, then without looking at the woman, motioned her to proceed. He walked back to the squad grinning all over his face; and once he got behind the wheel, he fairly ripped apart with laughter.

"What's so funny?" I asked, knowing he'd have to get a grip on himself before he could say anything. "She con you out of giving her a ticket?"

"Not exactly," he finally managed to say. "I just believed her story."

"*You* falling for a con job? You're losing your marbles."

The story that unfolded was so hilarious I convulsed along with Don when he told it. It seems the woman was in a mad rush for the bathroom and had been all the way from 54th. She was headed for 25th where she knew of a public restroom and we'd stopped her one block short of her urgent destination. When she was asked for her driver's license, her nervousness got the best of her and the bladder exploded with a vengeance.

"No wonder she was fidgety," I said. "But I'd have given her a ticket." I wouldn't have, of course, but I said so hoping to get a rise out of my partner.

He rose to the occasion. "Aww, come off it, Al," he said, bristling good naturedly. "You'd have let her go just like I did."

"Then I'm going to ticket *you*," I said jokingly.

"Me? What in blazes for?"

"Leaving the scene of an accident," I said.

He laughed at the trumped up charge, and we drove off conversing about the fortune a guy could make for coming up with a way to install emergency bathroom facilities in automobiles.

Every policeman could write a book of the excuses given him by drivers who get stopped for not obeying speed limits. And the strangest story given by any one officer could be topped by any other officer because there isn't any limit to the creative powers of the motorist in a spot.

I confess I've been conned out of giving tickets because the excuses were so doggoned original I fell for them. But there were other times ... take for instance, the case of straight-faced Charlie. I stopped him on 24th and Park after having followed him for several blocks. He'd been doing 50 in a 35 mile zone.

"You won't believe this," he said calmly when I asked why he was going so fast; and somehow, looking at his nondescript face with the pleading, innocent eyes, I thought I just well might.

"Try me," I offered.

"Well, he said apologetically as all get out, "it's such a strange darned thing I almost hate to tell you for fear you'll call me a liar."

By now my curiosity was piqued and I found myself in the ridiculous position of practically begging him to spit the story out. "Come on, Charlie, I'd like to hear it."

And out came the tall tale. It seems another squad had passed the innocent-but-honest Charlie when a $20 bill fell from the window. Knowing how much twenty dollars meant to the anything but well paid guardian of the public safety, Mr. Do-Good stopped to retrieve the prized portrait of Andrew Jackson and was speeding to catch the squad in a desperate effort to return it.

He then raised a moderately heavy question: it shouldn't be a crime for a guy to do a good deed, should it? There wasn't a trace of a grin on the man's face.

"You're right," I said finally, no grin on mine either.

His eyes brightened. "You mean I did the right thing?"

"No," I said and I was laughing now. "You're right. I don't believe you."

"Oh." Charlie was crestfallen.

"But your con job was so good I'm letting you off the hook," I said. Then I got serious and told him if I ever caught him speeding again, no con job in the world would get him out of a ticket. Did he understand?

"Yes, Sir," Charlie said, still poker faced. I waved him on.

"Keep the twenty bucks," I said magnamiously, "and buy yourself something real nice to go with your fancy story."

Even then Charlie didn't smile, but he did drive off, and I thought for a brief instant maybe I shouldn't have been so generous.

In addition to the incredible excuses for speeding, there were always the incredible offers of products, services and money in exchange for letting the admitted guilty go. The $50 on pay day. The set of tools in the trunk. The home made dinner every Wednesday for a month. Cocktails for two in an exotic place. And, of course, the age old offer to spend a night in bed with a voluptuous woman whose charms she'd guarantee would make any cop forget anything he wanted to forget.

I couldn't imagine accepting such bribes, nor did I ever succumb to the temptation, but there were policemen on occasion who did . . . often to their regret. Many whose ethical standards kept them from it for years, finally succumbed after having been worn down in the constant bombardment by public tempters.

The first time I met hapless Henry was on East 34th Street where we'd been called to check on a burglary. Before we stopped the squad, he ran up to us, jumped in the back seat and babbled drunkenly, "Take me to da slammer, Offishur; ah'm guilty."

The small black man was bleeding from a cut on the mouth and the blood dribbled down over a dirty, loose fitting tweed suit coat that had seen its better days before the wearer's time and had long since been separated from its matching trousers. Now and then the voluntary captive rubbed a frayed sleeve across his mouth and mumbled oaths at his assailant.

Don told him to shut up long enough to listen to a question and then try to anwer it.

He identified himself as Henry Logan.

"Address?"

"Don't live no place," he muttered. "Jush sort've hangs aroun'."

"How'd you get cut up?"

"Got schmacked by a 4 legged objeck come flyin' at me."

"You mean a cat? A dog?"

"A sh-shair, Man. Dis wile mamma picks up furnishur an' swings like she trainin' tigers."

"What were you doing in her apartment?"

"I wa'ant doin nothin an thass da plain truth."

We decided we'd check with the resident of the apartment to get the plain truth. Our back seat mumbler was obviously in no condition to tell it like it was.

We were met at the door by a husky black woman who looked as if she had just declared war on the entire neighborhood. "Ah want thet little black bastard behind bars," she screeched. "Efen ah evah sees him stealin mah staples agin ah'm goin choke him till he turn blue an drap daid."

"We've got him," I said. "Now tell us what happened."

She explained she'd come home to find a miserable stranger sitting at her table and eating from a sack of groceries she'd bought earlier.

"So what did you do then?"

"Ah done what any hard workin' pore woman woulda done then. Ah hit him ovah da haid with thet." She pointed to the cumbersome weapon, a paint chipped wooden chair, its legs wired together for support.

"This explains how he got the cut lip," Don said.

"Don't splain nothin cept mah aim," the woman said. "He fall an hit his dirty tater trap on thet toy truck."

"Had you seen this man before?" I asked, handing her the can of soup she'd beaned poor Henry with as he sprinted across the porch.

She took the can and examined it for dents. "Nevah laid eyes on him in mah life," she said forcefully. "Nevah hope ah do agin." She slammed the can on the table.

"Who called the police?"

There was no answer.

It didn't seem plausible that someone would break into a house to steal food, then sit at the table and eat it. More likely any food snatcher would take his loot elsewhere so that he could eat in peace without the risk of getting caught.

After further interrogation, we fit the puzzle together. The unfortunate thief actually was the woman's boyfriend of sorts and he had often pried the back door open when she was gone, making himself at home and helping himself to whatever he could find. This time, however, Henry had blown it and riled his mate beyond the point of clemency. He'd failed to clean up his mess.

"Thet free-loadin no good bum oughta do his wallowin' in a pig pen," she bellowed.

I scanned the surroundings. It looked as if the place had been struck by a tornado and ransacked by several burglars. The woman was obviously no housekeeper. I failed to see how she could have even noticed Henry hadn't put his left-over food away.

After having talked with Henry's attacker, I felt some sympathy for the poor man, but just what to do about it was a problem. I hated to book him for burglary but there wasn't much choice since a burglary *had* been reported and Henry *had* actually burglarized an apartment and stolen food. Besides, he needed a place to sleep off his drunk and I couldn't take him home without facing some repercussions from my own mate. Gayle was one understanding woman, but perhaps I, too, would push things to the point of chair throwing if I took advantage of her good nature and handed her this particular case.

So we took our ward to the fifth floor jail in the Hennepin County Court House where we booked him. We then found a sympathetic detective who said he'd let Henry sleep it off and let him go.

When it came time for the end of the month reports, Don and I had quite a discussion over the arrest. It bothered his conscience and mine to book the man for a felony; so since we'd had plenty of "valid" arrests that month, we compromised and called it a half-felony. The captain never asked us about it though no such indictment existed, and we were happy we didn't have to explain the charge.

We were not to be finished with the hapless burglar, however. Some time later we were called back to the house on 34th Street because a theft had been reported by the woman of the place. "Henry's at it again," Don said and I thought so, too . . . until we heard the story, that is.

The chair-throwing woman met us at the door and ushered us inside. "Some no 'count junkie ripped off the new bedroom set ah jus bought fer mah kids," she wailed. "Ah wanna report it and git mah money back."

Henry sat nodding his head in agreement to everything she detailed in the report though details were about as vague as instructions in a do-it-yourself assembly kit.

We listened to the story for some 20 confused minutes, then Don asked for a receipt of purchase. Naturally, she couldn't produce one. Henry rummaged through his pockets in an attempt to lend a convincing touch to the bogus search and his act was really quite good. It was not, however, convincing.

I finally called the "meeting" to order by telling the pair to shut up. "There isn't going to be any report made," I said. "And the reason is that you two never paid for a stick of furniture in your lives." I pointed to the counter full of empty bottles and beer cans. "There's where all your money goes. We know it and so do you."

The woman was indignant. "Why would ah call you cops to report mah stolen furniture efen ah didn' have none?'' she screamed, then began calling us names for being stupid.

"Because you want to report it to welfare so you can collect money on a bedroom set you never had.''

"Well, now Offishurs, you all know 'bout dis woman here . . .'' Henry began.

"Shet up or ah'll shet you up good,'' the woman said.

Henry looked like the cat that had just eaten a bird and been caught with a telltale feather in its mouth. He shut up.

We left the apartment with the woman thundering threats. She said she'd report us to everyone from the mayor to the paperboy. But we never heard about the matter again.

The woman's attempt to get money under false pretenses from welfare is one made by many people like her. Such con games are easily recognized by welfare authorities as well as by police officers. Even so, people like Henry and his woman never stop trying to pull one off.

"I had the feeling Henry would've told us the truth,'' I mused later when Don and I were having a lunch break. I remembered how pathetic he had looked when we left. He had shrugged his droopy shoulders, thrown up his hands and rolled his eyes as if to say, "What's a poor guy to do with a woman like that?''

Once again we assumed that to be the last we'd hear of hapless Henry and his vehement virago. Once again we were wrong. Several weeks later the call came to check an accident on East 34th. A pedestrian had been struck by a car.

"He just walked right into me,'' wailed the dazed motorist as he hovered over what he thought were the remains of a small black man who lay limp as a rag on the street.

Of course the victim was Hapless. More limp from booze than from injury but it did require a short hospital stay to get him mobile again.

Henry claimed it was an argument with thet woman which rendered him senseless enough to walk straight into traffic. "She enuf to drive a po' man to drink 'n get 'im kilt while she doin it," he moaned, thinking the vehicle had actually shoved him right through the pearly gates. What with the white walls, the clean, white bed and the white uniformed angels waiting on him hand and foot, Henry swore for three days he'd died and gone to heaven. Needless to say, he was one disappointed man when he learned he was still amongst the quick.

Henry's ambition after that ordeal was to be chauffered around in a white car. It seemed to him riding in clean, light comfort would bring his short-lived heaven back to earth—say nothing of its being considerably safer than staggering afoot.

And where there's a *will* there's a way. Henry actually achieved his ambition. On one glorious day it happened that he found himself the dumbfounded heir to $25,000, left by a distant well-shod relative whose ambition was to live to see the day Henry amounted to something. He couldn't wait that long, however, so instead he left a lump sum to expedite matters.

Henry worked fast. He spent it all in six weeks. He bought the car, a white '57 Chevrolet, hired a chauffeur and cruised about drinking the best hootch money could buy. He handed out hundred dollar bills to whoever would buy him a jug; and all the who-evers, knowing a good deal when they saw it, kept the change. Henry, too loaded to add and subtract, never knew the difference. Poor Henry. He just couldn't handle good luck. His programming was all wrong.

His woman *really* had it in for him after that. We found out just how much when we were called to check a domestic on East 34th.

"Here we go again," Don said. "It's the hapless wonder and his female tormentor."

The woman ran to meet us as we pulled up in front of the building. "Take thet nigger to jail," she screamed, pointing to the porch where a bruised and reeling Henry stood in the dim light.

"What did he do?"

"He raped me."

"When did he rape you?"

"Every day for the last five years," came the reply.

A thought went through me like an electric shock: Henry's torment must come to an end. I walked up to where the dazed creature stood looking like an hallucination in the flesh and said, "Henry, you're under arrest!"

Realizing I was up to something, Don went along with the act. He pulled out his miranda card to advise the stupefied Mr. Logan of his rights. He could remain silent. Anything he said could be used against him. He had the right to an attorney. If he couldn't afford to hire one, the court would provide one. Did he have anything to say?

For once even the woman was silent.

After a long pause, Henry blinked, scratched his head and waved his hands as if to clear away the foggy haze which enveloped his clouded brain. "Forgive me, Offishur," he managed to say, "but why is ah bein 'rested?"

It *was* a good question ... probably one of the more intelligent ones he'd ever asked.

For a split second I floundered. Then, summoning the creative powers which come to motorists in a jam, the words popped into my head. I cleared my throat, adopted a serious pose and took a deep breath to get the resonance of authority in my voice. "Henry," I said with gravity, "the charge is First Degree Mopery with Intent to Creep."

He slumped. We took him by the arms and led him to the squad. He said nothing but the look in his eyes spoke of this as being the ultimate, the coup de grâce ... the blow to end all blows and the one from which he'd never recover.

On the way downtown I told Henry of the seriousness of his crime. He seemed willing to listen.

"What kin ah do, Offishur? Jush name it. Anythin you ask ta git dis monkey offa mah back."

"All right," I said, "we'll just stop to have a good long chat over a cup of coffee. If you'll tell us what holdup men are working this area, we'll let you go free."

The man agreed. We stopped for coffee. But trying to get reasonable answers from a drunk is like trying to converse with a foreigner when you don't know the language. Henry didn't know a holdup man from the man in the moon. Obviously, we were wasting our time.

"Henry," Don said, "you can split. We're not going to take you in."

Henry's sad eyes brightened. He thanked us profusely and started for the door. Then he turned and came back to us with the big question uppermost in his mesmerised mind. "Jush what is Mopery?"

"Don't worry about it," I said. "We're not going to charge you with it after all."

And that was the last of our encounters with hapless Henry. To this day he probably doesn't know what *mopery* means.

According to the dictionary, *mope* means "to act

in a dazed or stupid manner or to give oneself up to dull or dejected brooding, or to move slowly or aimlessly." I prided myself on the inspiration of the moment which gave me a term that fit hapless Henry so perfectly. Perhaps the "intent to creep" was inspired also since, had Henry taken one more drink, I'm certain he'd have been unable to walk upright and would have had to resort to crawling on all fours.

I thought about Henry often after that. We had rescued him from the clutches of the woman; and so far as we knew, that was the end of their relationship. On occasion, I could see Henry in my mind's eye as a sober, God fearing man with a determined walk and a purpose in life. And always the picture would lead me to pray with more determination about God's direction in my life. I asked Him to open doors.

And after one of those prayers, He opened a door. I learned, at long last, what God's real purpose for police officers is.

Chapter VII

The Purpose

I sat in the study reading my Bible and thinking of the tremendous power packed between its covers. It contained the way of salvation for me and for all men. It contained the creed by which I had tried to live ever since I surrendered my life to Christ some ten years before. It contained the words of hope which had lifted me up whenever I felt discouraged. It contained the guidelines I needed whenever I wondered which course to take and those occasions were many. And while I could quote many of the Book's passages verbatim, the messages were always new. And while I thought I understood what was meant, even in some of the complex passages, there were always fresh insights given when I sought for them in earnest and even when I didn't. No wonder really. The Bible is the "word of God." I could say that phrase perfunctorily and reaffirm it routinely, but whenever I *really* stopped to think about it, the magnitude of those words would overwhelm me. *The word of God.* What a document!

When He sometimes seemed far away, it was reassuring to remember His word was right at my fingertips. No need to research volumes in public libraries to find what the great men said about infinity. Here was infinity spoken by the Infinite One. No need to send away for materials in order to complete a study on God's purpose for mankind. Here was the source of all material. No need to ask around for opinions from so-called authorities and try to sift the meaning from conflicting reports. Here was *the* authority. No need to travel the world in search of truth from learned philosophers and inspired sages. Here was truth from the Omnipotent, the Omnipresent, the Omniscient. Universal yet individual. As old as the beginning of time and as new as tomorrow.

I had just read a portion of the Psalms when I sat thinking about the dynamic content of the book I held in my hands. For some reason I opened the word of God once more and my eyes noted verse 4 of Paul's letter to the Romans, chapter 13. Obviously the selection was not made at random for what I saw startled me and I sat upright as though I'd been thunderstruck. It was as if I'd been blind and the scales had suddenly fallen from my eyes. I could see!

In talking about rulers in positions of authority, Paul was saying, "For he is the minister of God to thee for good. But if thou do that which is evil, be afraid; for he beareth not the sword in vain: for he is the minister of God, a revenger to execute wrath upon him that doeth evil."

Now two words in that passage were hitting me: *sword* and *minister*. In Bible school I had learned to take key words and study other places in scripture where the words were used in an attempt to get God's attitude on the subject. In police work I had learned to gather all the possible clues I could find on a matter, then piece them together and build a case.

I began my detective work.

I found the word *sword* is used 38 times in the Bible. Often it refers to the word of God but here it doesn't. It is simply a weapon and it's used independently ... that is, it doesn't tie in to any other reference in scripture.

I found the word *minister* stated as *servant* in other translations and the word *minister* is used hundreds of times, always in reference to serving or helping the people; so it seemed logical that the two words were interchangeable.

I wondered if policemen could legitimately be included among those in positions of authority and I decided they could. In fact, I found that the J.B. Phillips translation uses the word *policemen* instead of *ruler* and so does the Living Bible. That discovery was electrifying! Paul was talking about me, a street cop!

Of course, the word in those days wasn't *policeman* or *cop*. Such men were called centurions or soldiers. Actually, the centurion was one in charge of many soldiers just as today's police captain is in charge of many officers. It was the individual soldier who was the street cop.

And here God was calling those soldiers and those of us who are street cops, *ministers*! And I wasn't bearing or toting the .357 magnum in vain! The sword in those days was the defensive weapon just as the gun is today and when I substituted that word *magnum*, the message really hit home! My heart pounded as it dawned on me that here was the answer to the question I'd been asking for years! Yes, I was a cop. Yes, I was a minister. There was no conflict of interest whatsoever! What's more, my authority was derived from God! *He* placed me in my position. I didn't have to wonder any more whether or not I was doing what He wanted me to do. I was!

My job as a cop was to be, first of all, a minister. Then, if the people didn't respond, I was to get tough ... to use bodily force or the weapon if necessary. But even in so doing, I would *still* be a minister! Because this passage very clearly points out that first "... he is a minister of God ... for good," and secondly that "... he is a minister of God, a revenger to execute wrath ... " What a revelation *that* was ... what a relief ... to know that we, the pistol packing "revengers," were ministers of God, too!

I wanted to talk to someone else about what had just been revealed to me. I knew God had spoken. I knew what I'd been shown was truth; but, eager to share the revelation as well as to get further affirmation of it, I decided to get together with John Owen, a minister friend of mine and quite a scholar when it comes to researching the scriptures. Not only did he agree fully with what I shared, but he gave me further insights which excited me all the more. Before I get into those, however, there follows the text from Romans taken from the revised standard version which John prefers to use:

"Let every person be subject to the governing authorities for there is no authority except from God, and those that exist have been put there by God. Therefore, he who resists the authority resists what God has appointed, and those who resist will incur judgment. The rulers are not a terror to good conduct, but to bad. Would you have no fear of him who is an authority? Then do what is good and you will receive his approval for he is God's servant for your good. But if you do evil, be afraid for he does not bear the sword in vain. He is the servant of God to execute His wrath upon the wrongdoer; therefore, one must be subject, not only to avoid God's wrath, but also for the sake of conscience."

John pointed out other passages in the New Testament that deal with the relationship of people to those in authority and I quote those here also:

"Remind them to be submissive to rulers and authorities, to be obedient, to be ready for any honest work, to speak evil of no one, avoid quarreling, to be gentle and to show a perfect courtesy to all men." Titus 3:1-2.

"First of all, then, I urge supplications, prayers, intercessions and thanksgivings be made for all men, for kings and all who are in high positions that we may lead a quiet, peaceable life, godly and respectful in every way. This is good and it is acceptable in the sight of God, our savior. He desires all men to be saved and to come to the knowledge of the truth." I Timothy 2:1-4.

"Be subject for the Lord's sake to every human institution. Whether it be to the emperor as supreme or to governors as sent by Him to punish those who do wrong and to praise those who do right. For it is God's will that by doing right you should put to silence the ignorance of foolish men. Live as free men, yet without using your freedom as a pretext for evil, but live as servants of God. Honor all men, love the brotherhood, fear God, honor the emperor." I Peter 2:13-17.

All these verses deal with the concept of authority and the word that's translated *ruler* ... especially in Romans 13 and in I Peter—can very legitimately be translated *police officer* as it is in the J. B. Phillips translation and in the Living Bible. The word *minister*, which is also translated *servant*, is particularly significant. Both words are derived from the Greek word *diakonos*; so in a very real sense, they are the same. And the word *diakonos* is the word from which *deacon* is derived. In some churches deacons are ordained to serve the body of Christ. It's their function to minister to the church along with the pastor in capacities for its good, for its protection and for its nurture. "I take this passage to mean," John said, "that a police officer is to society what a deacon is to the church. And it's clear from this passage that no person is exempt from governing authorities and that Paul makes no attempt to indicate whether these people in authority are born of God's spirit or not."

Paul assumes, as do many of the other writers, that God is able to work through governing authorities whether or not they are submissive to Him. John went on to explain how this demonstrated the wonderful redemptive ability of God in that He uses *all* men in positions of authority to further His purpose ... whether or not they are Christians. Of course, His ultimate purpose is to unite all things in Christ ... things in heaven and things on earth.

John agreed that the context of this passage is especially important to police officers because it shows their function in today's society is to enforce the law and to deter crime as well as to apprehend criminals. They are to approve good conduct, true, but they also serve to strike fear or terror in those who do bad. They are given the right to "thump" the wrongdoers ... to straighten them out with force if necessary. But they are ministers whether they are approving good conduct or revenging bad conduct.

I asked how that idea squared with the passage in Matthew which tells a person to turn the other cheek if the enemy strikes him.

"I think it all depends on whether that person is protecting himself or someone else," John replied.

"If you're concerned about yourself alone, you've got a choice. You can decide if you're going to let a guy thump you and get away with it (if you feel God's purpose would be better served to do that), or whether you're going to fight back. But when someone threatens another, or threatens society, you don't really have a choice . . . not if you're a cop. You're going to protect that person from being beaten because that's your job. And you don't have to think twice about it because God says it's your responsibility to protect him and He has given you the right to do it. He's placed you in that position of authority and you derive your power from Him.

"If police officers could just latch on to that concept. But the great tragedy is, of course, that so many are called to serve and they don't have the spiritual resources from within to fulfill the task to which they're called. Another sad situation is that of those who *are* Christians, so many don't understand fully what their rights and responsibilities are so they go around feeling guilty about packing firearms. 'How can I be a police officer and be a Christian at the same time?' they ask.

"Well, my answer to them is, 'God appoints you to protect His people and you can't be a police officer *without* being a Christian . . . not the kind of cop He wants you to be anyway.' Police officers are supposed to be Christians. It's part of Holy Writ. They have the right to punish, the right to correct, the right to enforce the law. They have the right to pack a 'sword' and they better well use it if it's necessary because God commissions them to use it. They are first and foremost God's revengers . . . not their own and not society's.

"That may be difficult to accept, but it would be easier if those in authority fully understood what is meant by derived power...where it's derived *from*. Their positions aren't simply civil service positions granted by the state for passing a test. They're not appointive positions granted by human authorities; they're not elective positions granted by the public they serve. Not initially, that is. They are positions granted by God and those who receive them are His servants, His ministers. Quite a responsibility! But it's encouraging to know that the recipient of such authority, perhaps more than other persons, experiences grace—that unmerited favor of God's goodness, of His approval.

"And because he experiences such grace, he ought all the more to respond willingly, out of love to God and to his fellow man, by being obedient to follow His orders."

It seemed to me that if everybody caught on to this particular message, God's kingdom would surely come to earth in a hurry. Especially if those who respond to authority would do it in the way *they* are commissioned...to be courteous, for example. Not to resist authority as so many do, but to be obedient to it. And if they'd make "supplications, prayers, intercessions and thanksgivings" for those in authority, we could truly live as God intends which is as free men, "not using freedom as a pretext for evil."

After hearing what John had to say, I felt as though I had enough ammunition to take on the entire criminal world. I was eager to test that ammunition and I did so the first chance I had.

When Don and I were called to a domestic one night, I told him my plan. "You gotta be kidding," he said.

The argument between this particular man and wife was not their first. They'd been going at it hot and heavy for years and I felt certain these arguments were ready to peak at the stage of violence. "Look, Don," I said, "all this other shoot 'em up, kick 'em, stomp on 'em, take 'em to jail...that stuff doesn't work. I'm going to try something different. City never said I couldn't."

"Well, I don't care what you do," he said finally, "so long as it works." He agreed the tough talk, the jailing, whatever, wasn't effective and he didn't have any better suggestions he said.

"OK then," I said, "just let me handle it and see what happens."

We walked into the room. The tension was so thick you could feel it. Hatred was personified in those people. It came out in words...it showed in their eyes...it evidenced itself in bodily movement. They obviously abhorred each other and with a passion.

"Sit down, both of you," I commanded. Surprisingly, they sat. They looked at me wondering what I was going to say and with a glare that told me whatever it was, it wasn't going to work.

"You two need to surrender your lives to Christ," I said simply.

They looked stunned...as if they hadn't heard correctly.

"Come again," the man said, "we need to *what*?"

"You need to surrender your lives to Jesus Christ," I repeated. "That's the only way you're going to quit fighting and learn how to love instead of hate."

"What's going on?" the man said. "I thought you were a cop, not a preacher."

"We don't need any lousy religion," the woman said.

But as I explained why I felt it was important

to them ... how they were suffering from burdens God never intended for them to bear, they listened quietly. And the outcome was that they agreed I could line up a minister from whom they'd seek counseling. Now, I don't know whether or not the final chapter is written to that story, but I do know we were never called back to that place and I know that the seed was planted and that God nurtures the seeds we plant.

I tried that approach, oh, probably ten different times in domestics. Sometimes I even prayed with the people, sometimes laid hands on them. Don would look at me and shake his head as if to say, "Oh, no, not again," but his attitude was really that if it worked, he didn't care. He never tried to keep me from it. Once he got used to the idea he even joked about it. "I'll carry the shot gun in case they don't respond," he'd say, "and you carry the Bible."

I told him that made good sense because the Bible is a powerful weapon in itself. I quoted Hebrews 4:12. "The word of God is quick and powerful, and sharper than any two edged sword, piercing even to the dividing asunder of soul and spirit, and of the joints and marrow, and is a discerner of the thoughts and intents of the heart." That quotation interested him.

The beautiful thing about it all was, of course, that it *did* work. I had tested it out and *proved* that it worked. "Now," I thought, "if I could just get the rest of the guys to get a hold on this, we'd be dynamite. We'd *really* make some inroads in this business of crime stopping."

I decided to take a good, long in-depth look at the ten men in my unit in an attempt to determine my best approach in telling them what I had learned.

Chapter VIII

The Jesters

Les Carnahan and J. T. Robins, the duo that rode squad 641, sometimes worked the power shift in low gear. From 7 p.m. to 3 a.m.—high crime time—they patrolled an easy, quiet residential district where there was seldom any high crime to deal with. They preferred it that way. If anything heavy did come up, there were occasions when finding these two guys in order to handle it took a better detective than the sergeant had on his force.

Carnahan was big and he was tough. He stood 6'3", a muscular 240 pounder—dark haired, some 45 years old and handsome as they come. Hands big enough to choke a grizzly. He looked great in uniform when the uniform didn't look as though it'd been slept in, and every now and then it looked that way because every now and then Carn slept in it.

His partner in crime-stopping was J. T. Robins, whose real name was Jesse but he hated it and pre-ferred being called J.T. which possessed the conno-tations of masculinity he thought his appearance lacked. But everybody called him Round Robin since a goodly number of the 200 pounds which draped his 6 foot frame were bulged above the belt line. He'd have looked great in a Santa Claus suit and he'd have made a hit with kids of all ages because J. T. was one likeable guy.

Carn and Round Robin could handle anything there was to handle in the way of cop work and when they did take on heavy action, they were all business. But in routine assignments, they were pleasant, amiable guys with a ready story to tell that kept people laughing. We called them The Jesters.

Everybody razzed them about having three major concerns which preempted any call to arms: snoozing, snacking and smoking.

After someone once discovered feather pillows in the trunk of their squad, they were jokingly accused of wheeling 641 to a different hide-away-bed every night. While the accusation was exaggerated, there was an element of truth in it.

The sergeant took the joking so seriously he'd blow his stack every time he needed this team and couldn't find them. Sometimes when he wasn't busy after midnight, he'd take it upon himself to play sleeper sleuth and check every place he could think of to locate his boys: construction sites, factories, car lots and he'd never tell you where else. "If I ever find those pillow packers," he'd threaten, "I'll ram the damn feathers down their throats and can 'em on the spot!"

But he never found them for Carn and Round Robin were masters at eluding the Sarge and masters at parking 641 where it couldn't be seen.

The Jesters were also accused of being preoccupied with fire. Carn smoked a cigar—Round Robin a pipe and they were forever stoking the dying embers. Their squad was littered with the paraphernalia needed for their habit: boxes of cigars, lighters, matches, pipe cleaners, lighter fluid, pouches, tobacco cans and the like. Carn clipped a big clothespin to his ashtray and used the open ends to hold his cigar butts.

Round Robin was always removing it so that he could rap his pipe against the tray, then he'd forget to put it back where it belonged. The two were forever rummaging around for that clothespin. We went out and bought them a package of the things one time and clipped a dozen each to the rims of their hats.

Everybody liked The Jesters including the citizens in their district. They rarely wrote traffic tags, they made few arrests. Laughing and joking, seldom taking life seriously, they were the good humor boys of the force.

They knew the right places for Code 7 (the "professional" term for coffee break) so if anybody wanted to know where to get the best wire water for the cheapest prices, he asked The Jesters. Code 7 was the third concern they were accused of being preoccupied with.

But Carn and Round Robin were excellent policemen. There were times one of them could do a job the so called expert couldn't, and times they could handle a job six policemen combined couldn't take care of.

One particular night some 20 squads were pursuing men who had been involved in the armed robbery of a super market. When one officer saw them dash into a building on 32nd and Garfield, the Flying Squad was called. Like the well known SWAT teams of television fame, these men took care of heavy stuff and were the cream of the crop so far as training and skill were concerned. When the thieves refused to open the door, the Squad's karate expert decided to do it in with one of his well aimed chops. He strode across the hall for ample running room and, lunging forward with the speed of a champion race horse, slammed into the barrier. Nothing happened. He lunged again. Again nothing happened. Carnahan watched the procedure as it was repeated several times without result, then stepped up to the exhausted professional and said casually, "Why don't you let *me* try it?"

The man stared at Carn with a tougher-than-thou glint in his eyes, then stepped aside as if to say, "Be my guest and make an ass of yourself."

But when the mighty bull charged, all questions of who's tougher were answered once and for all time. In one shattering second, hinges, splinters, bolts and nuts flew every which way, one hitting the stunned karate expert whose eyes bulged with disbelief. The modern Joshua had fit the battle of Jericho with no more apparent effort than it would have taken to blow a trumpet.

Jesse T. Robins was no slouch either when it came to putting a quick end to a heavy problem. I witnessed him in action one night and I admit I was proud of the way he took care of things. Two officers were having a hard time subduing a mugger and they wrestled on the ground with him for five minutes, unable to get the man handcuffed and into the squad. He was a heavyweight, strong and agile, and he knew how to handle himself in hand to hand combat.

J. T. slapped my back, said, "Come on, let's take care of it for 'em," and walked into the middle of the action.

"You guys been getting dirty long enough," he said to his fellow officers. And with that he picked the man up as if he were a chihuahua pup, slammed him on top the squad car, handcuffed him, threw him into the back seat and walked away. He hadn't needed my help at all.

I admired The Jesters. I liked them. But they seemed so nonchalant in their approach to police work and to life in general, I doubted they'd take me seriously if I told them cops were supposed to be ministers. No doubt they'd think I was joking and say something like, "Palmquist, you gotta be going for laughs."

OVER AND OUT

Sid Overgaard and Herb Swarthout were naturally called the Over and Out team. They took their jobs seriously, sometimes too much so, and they prided themselves on being unpopular.

They patrolled a district from Lake Street to 38th and from Lyndale to Chicago, an area heavily concentrated with blacks which was unfortunate for the blacks because Sid Overgaard hated them. But he was impartial. He hated Chicanos too. And Norwegians. And Swedes. And Indians. His creed: All men are created equal and ought to be treated that way.

He reminded me of the central figure in one of his favorite stories—actually his only story and he told it without laughing because Sid just didn't think anything was funny, including his own humor.

A man went into a gun shop and asked for the best high powered rifle he could buy. And the most expensive scope. And 20,000 rounds of ammunition. "What are you going to do with this?" the proprietor asked.

"Shoot cans," came the reply.

"Cans? You don't need all this costly equipment just to shoot cans."

"Yes, I do," the man affirmed.

"For the luva Mike, what kind of cans do you intend to shoot?"

"Ameri-cans, Mexi-cans, Afri-cans, Angli-cans . . ."

Other than the first time he told that story, Sid Overgaard was somewhat of a bore. He considered himself extremely professional, which he was, and he took great pains to enforce the law in every minute detail. His associates went out of their way to avoid getting into discussions with him because he was forever pointing out where they fell short or missed the mark in carrying out their duties. If anybody disagreed with him, he'd walk off in a tri-colored snit and nobody could humor him out of it.

Another six footer, husky and strong, Sid sported a neatly trimmed moustache, was impeccable in his dress, and strutted about in spit shined shoes that fairly glistened in the dark. He spit shined his badge, too, though he'd deny it if you accused him of it.

At thirty-seven, Sid had been on the force for twelve years and was still bucking for a promotion. The longer he waited the tougher he got. But for some reason he was always passed on by when the promos were handed out. He attributed that to his being so effective where he was they couldn't do without him and he could have been right.

His cohort, Swarthout, was super bright. Twenty-four, college grad, brand new in the department, he was gung ho from go. Though he called himself a self-made man, it was obvious he took a few lessons in how to hate the world from his elder partner. He wore large horn rimmed glasses which somehow gave him a look of perpetual surprise. He, too, referred to the people on the street as slobs and saw each one as a potential criminal. He, too, was somewhat of a bore but he carried it one step further: he rankled everybody around him with his cockiness. We often called him the Horn Rimmed Upstart. Always getting his feathers ruffled over something.

But he was smart and he knew the rules in his code book. He was out to save the world from the slobs and one way to get it done was to make arrests for everything the code book said you could arrest people for. Another was to write traffic tickets. No matter how minor the infraction and hang the mitigating circumstances. So the motor died in mid-intersection. It so happens you can't park in mid-traffic.

I rode with Swarthout while his partner was on vacation and I soon found out it was a man sized job to keep him in line. We pulled a fellow over on 28th and First because of a minor infraction; and when I got out to talk to him about it, he started to pull ahead in an attempt to get out of the line of traffic. Herb, upon seeing the man make a move, got so excited he gunned the squad ahead and nearly rammed the guy's car which in turn forced him up on the curb. That did it. Herb jumped out, leaped at the surprised motorist, pulled him out from behind the wheel and slammed him against the squad. "Brother, there's no way you're going to escape," he screeched, his voice coming out in a shaky falsetto.

The man was too shocked and too frightened to speak.

I calmed Herb down and sent him back to the squad. "Just cool it," I said, "and wait for me. I'll handle this."

"The guy's a maniac," the motorist gasped.

I then calmed *him* down, apologized for the roughing and sent him on his way.

Swarthout was disappointed I hadn't issued a ticket. At that time, the captain of our precinct recommended each team write approximately 40 tickets a month. That's one per man per working shift. Herb wanted to make sure he wrote more than his quota just to impress upon the captain that he was willing to go above and beyond the call of duty.

The recommended quota no longer exists... probably because guys like Swarthout didn't know how to handle a suggestion with good sense.

There was a humorous streak on the flip side of Herb Swarthout, however. Not one *he* recognized as funny, but the rest of us did. His vocabulary was expansive and he used big words with an air of superiority. Nothing pleased him more than being pedantic to the point where nobody understood what he was talking about. Unless it was somebody's asking what in the world he meant so he could explain it.

I guess the word that most accurately describes him is *pedant*: "one who pays undue attention to book learning and formal rules without having an understanding or experience in practical affairs." Swarthout could read books but not people.

But getting back to the flip side. As if in attempt to offset his abrasive qualities and be one of the boys, he always used the in-word of the day. Or tried to. Almost without fail he botched it. When "groovy" was in, he called it "gravey," and Overgaard would correct him. What people referred to as "gross" Swarthout referred to as "grouse." If a crime had us buffaloed, it had Sid baffleoed.

But the day he told the street gang he'd had it with the trouble they caused—that he was hissed off to put it in their vernacular—they almost broke his eardrums with their piercing "s" sounds. He told them to freeze it but they didn't hear him.

"What in the name of common sense were they hissing for?" he asked his partner later. "I say something wrong?"

"Yeah, but don't ask me to explain it," Sid replied.

Herb wasn't about to let the matter drop. "I insist you tell me if you know," he said.

So Sid told him. " . . . and another thing is," he added, "you're supposed to say cool it, not freeze it."

And Herb said "Oh" as if he understood but he really didn't. At least that's the way Sid told it.

I knew if I even suggested to the Over and Out team that God had a better way to deal with street problems, they'd have looked upon me as some sort of crazy reactionary who definitely needed to be put under surveilance.

Chapter IX

The Hardy Boys

Cliff Hartman and Vic Rendahl dressed in street clothes and rode an unmarked squad. Their duty was to scout the entire area of South Minneapolis in what's called aggressive routine patrol.

Teams in marked squads have definite patrol boundaries and take assignments from the dispatcher in their precinct who, upon getting reports from the public, decides which men to deport to the spot and notifies them by radio. Teams in unmarked cars generally have patrol boundaries also and are assigned specific marked squads which they're to help. They're radioed when those squads are busy and/ or when they need back up power on heavy stuff.

Teams in aggressive routine patrol, however, come under different regulations. They're not to get calls from the dispatcher. They're not given specific squads to back up. They don't have district boundaries. They're strictly on their own to snoop out trouble that isn't reported and to take care of it. They are expected, of course, to roust it out with a fair amount of frequency and the Hartman-Rendahl team did. We often called them the Hardy Boys whose fabled action-packed lives never fail to intrigue the kids who read that series.

It was difficult for us to think of the guys as separate individuals since they seemed so much alike. Both were good looking young men about twenty-seven years old. Both some over six feet tall. Both meticulous in the way they dressed and in the way they conducted themselves. They were fine officers and generally quite easy to work with. They weren't super brutal or overly pleasant; somehow they seemed to strike a good balance which a lot of cops are never able to do.

They had one hang-up, however. They didn't like getting hung up on petty stuff. It crimped the style to which they'd become accustomed. Regardless of the no-call rule, there were times they had to be called . . . times when there weren't other squads available; and when the dispatcher asked them to check a broken window or whatever, they'd hit the roof. And when the sergeant found out about it, *he'd* hit the roof. "We oughta put those white collar comics in a marked car and swamp 'em with all the cotton pickin' petty crap that comes in," he'd say. "They never turn up anything anyway."

And when he'd say it, someone would always remind him that Hartman and Rendahl had quite a record of good arrests each month.

"You drive around all night, every night with nothing to do, and a crook is bound to run into the side of your squad or something," he'd counter. "It's the odds."

But the truth was these two officers had a nose for trouble and they zeroed in on it with amazing frequency. The Sarge knew it, too, and he never openly voiced his irritation to them.

I was in trouble one night and they found me

when nobody else could. All the cops in South Minneapolis were thankful for that, but it left me chagrined because I had no idea there was a problem and how serious it was or could have been. That was the night I screwed up things good.

Early in my career as a police officer I sometimes worked the mobile beat. That is, I rode a motor scooter from one block to another. I'd park it and walk around as a sort of security blanket for store keepers and shoppers in the area, then scoot off to another block. On this night there wasn't much going on so I decided I'd putt around looking for stolen cars, one in particular. I thought I spotted it so I took the radio mike off its stand, depressed the button and called the dispatcher for a license check. Failing to turn up anything, I replaced the mike and forgot to release the button. Now, that may seem insignificant, but it meant every squad car in the area had such a whale of a lot of static they could neither take nor make calls.

Hartman and Rendahl decided to forego crook catching that night and go after the dumb cop who had his mike stuck. Of course, there was no way to tell which kook it was or where he was located, but that didn't stop this team. It took awhile, but they found me.

"Look, Rookie," Cliff said condescendingly, "do you realize you fouled up the entire communications system in South Minneapolis for two hours?"

"Do you have any idea of the seriousness of that?" his partner added.

I realized fully what the implications of my oversight were but that didn't stop the guys from spelling them out for me. Needless to say, I got to be a fanatic about releasing the mike button after that.

For a long time the Hardy Boys looked upon me

as a dumb klutz and it wasn't until the tables were turned that I gained some respect in their eyes. Actually it wasn't so much respect as it was the clout of having one up on them so to speak.

We had an artful con man in the area who made a comfortable living rolling drunks. He'd go into bars, find a well stewed prune, get friendly with him and wheedle an invitation to his house where he'd clobber him, take his wad and scram. Nobody could catch him at it.

I saw him go into a bar one night so I staked the place out which means I sat across the street in an unmarked car and watched. Sure enough he eventually came out and with what appeared to be the best friend he ever had. I put out a call for help and followed them to the unsuspecting inebriate's apartment. As I stood outside the door waiting for the appropriate moment to storm in, my back up unit arrived. It was Hartman and Rendahl. Obviously, I had the situation under control but they took over, telling me all the things I already knew.

"Now we can't go in there too soon," Cliff advised me.

"Got to wait til the guy assaults so we've got a case on our hands," Vic elaborated.

"Could get ourselves in a pack of trouble if we haven't got a case," Cliff said.

I listened. These guys had been on the force longer than I had and I figured they knew more than I did, so I nodded my head in agreement to everything they said. But when Cliff decided the time for crashing in had come, I had to voice my objections. "It's too soon, Cliff," I said. "Nothing's happened yet."

That's all it took to ruffle the feathers of the super crime aggressors. "Look, Rookie," Cliff said, "We've been around awhile. We know what we're doing."

"But I'm telling you, nothing's hap . . ."

"Stand back and watch," Vic interrupted. "You might learn something."

With that they rammed the door and barged in only to find the con man and his host chatting amiably.

Now there's nothing more pathetic than the expression on the face of a cop who's loused up a heavy deal in front of his would-be suspects. He's surprised as all get out but he can't show it. He's disappointed as a penniless kid in a candy store but he can't say so. He feels like an idiot but he's got to pretend he isn't even though he just acted like one. He's got to maintain his dignity even though he just blew it; and he's got to think of something fast because he's violated somebody's constitutional rights and he'll be in a heap of trouble if a law suit is slapped against him.

To make things worse for these particular veterans, they've got a rookie standing behind them who's curious to learn how they're going to handle the matter from here on out. I wasn't saying "I told you so," but they knew what I was thinking and they could see I was having a tough time to keep from laughing. They could also sense I was disgusted for their having blown my bust.

So they did the only thing they could do: apologize and offer an explanation, feeble though it was. They then made an attempt at reparation. "Look," Cliff said to the drunk who, fortunately, was too happily saturated to much care one way or the other, "we'll send somebody out to fix your door."

"I'd preeshiate it," he drooled pleasantly and we scrambled out of there like kids who'd just been told to switch from cops to robbers. Lucky for us no complaints were filed and no charges pressed.

Hartman and Rendahl weren't the kind of guys who'd be interested in knowing that God was calling them to be ministers. I knew if I tried to tell them they'd say, "Look, Rookie, we know what our assignment is and we're not to take calls from *anybody.*"

THE TAG TEAM

Doug Moore and Louie Comstock were the kind of guys you'd never notice in a crowd, not even a small crowd. Those who never forget a name would have forgotten the names of Moore and Comstock. Those who never forget a face would have made an exception with these two. But deck them out in uniform and put them in a squad car and everybody for miles around knew who they were. No doubt they'd had an encounter with one or both of these cops at one time or another.

These men had a thing about writing traffic tickets. We used to tell them they'd tag their own wives on the way to the hospital with one of the kids. Or their own grandmothers jaywalking to ditch a mugger. We believe they would have, too.

Moore wanted to be known as a big, tough cop, but unfortunately he was only about 5'9" and of very slight build. A sort've little fellow with a tremendous desire to make himself conspicuous by his presence. I would imagine he was twenty-four or five. His partner was a couple years older, a couple inches taller and usually a couple steps behind when it came time to head for the action afoot.

They patrolled a district bordered by Freeway 35 on the east, Lyndale Avenue on the west, Franklin Avenue on the north and 32nd Street on the south—an area of about five square miles close to downtown Minneapolis and populated by some 50,000 people, most of them living in apartments.

Thirty or forty years ago this area was the swank residential district of the elite: the corporate executives, the industrial tycoons and those who comprised the uppermost echelon of the upper class. Then blacks and other minorities started moving in and in those days that was anathema. The homeowners with foresight sold out and headed for the suburbs. Those with hindsight waited too long and found their property devalued so much it wasn't economically feasible for them to join the exodus. So they put up and shut up, or at least tried to.

The once beautiful homes were converted into not so beautiful apartment houses and eventually thousands of freedom seeking singles, graduates from parental authority in the small towns around The Cities, swarmed in. What with the minorities already there, they created a majority of noise makers who partied at the drop of a bottle cap.

And at the hint of complaints from natives who could no longer shut up, Moore and Comstock would crash the parties, pack the loud mouths in the paddy wagon and haul them off of jail.

Sometimes they were so eager to get the job done they'd forget about the city ordinance which prohibits loud parties after 10 o'clock and they'd shut them down by 8:30 or so. Nobody on the force complained much about it. Most cops hated the wild party detail and Moore and Comstock were two of them.

What they really liked to do was the thing they had a thing about: write traffic tags. And they left no margin for mercy. If you were seen with a wheel over the center line for one split second, you'd be tagged even if you had swerved to miss a gopher in a chuck hole.

The team was generous though. If patrolmen in

the district southwest of them couldn't meet the recommended quota of 20 tags per individual a month—
and that happened often since the area was quiet
and there just weren't that many offenses to go
around—the Tag Team would give them some of
theirs. It wasn't unusual for them to write 15 tickets
in one night. They seemed to feel an obligation to
help everybody else meet *their* obligations . . . especially Moore.

I worked with him one night and got a good picture of how hype he was on tagging. We were head-
ing down Lyndale from 24th when we saw a car
zooming straight for us. Just before what would have
been a horrible head on collision and probably cur-
tains for us, the driver careened east on 22nd and
rammed into a parked car. I jumped out to see if
the guy was hurt and when I did, he backed away
from the smashed vehicle and started toward me.
I jumped to the side, reached in and pulled him
right out through the window. I rough-housed him
a bit to slap handcuffs on him but it was necessary.
Now we were in an area full of long-haired, anti-
establishment hippies; and while nobody saw me jerk
the guy out of the window, there was an audience
of a hundred or more by the time I got him out
and away from his car. And Moore paid no attention
to me whatsoever because he was busy counting
traffic violations.

"1. broken tail lights . . . 2. broken headlights . . .
3. driving under the influence . . ."

Meanwhile, I arrested the character and strange
though it may seem, *and* as untimely, while I was
leading him to the squad, he slumped in a dead
faint.

Now my audience *did* see that and assumed I
had thumped him. They got into the act and began

to scream and I mean loud. "Police brutality, pig, dirty blankety blank cop." What's more, there were rumbles of threatened violence that forecast nothing short of a bloody riot.

And all the while Moore kept on counting. "15. license light out . . . 16. muffler violation . . . 17. open bottle . . . 18. over center line . . ."

"Hey, Doug," I said desperately, "we've gotta split this scene like now!"

"24. failure to obey police officer . . . 25. incorrect address . . ."

We got out of there when he got to 26 and to this day I don't think he realizes the drama that unfolded before him that night though he's probably told his side of the story a hundred times.

It didn't seem to me either member of the Tag Team would be interested in being a minister for the Lord, but I would have liked to share the idea with them. Trouble is, I knew they'd have been as oblivious to what I said as Moore was to what I did the night he wrote 26 tags in one fell swoop.

Chapter X

The Attorneys

Gene Lapinski and Ed Giles were law officers to the letter of it. They liked any kind of action they could get which was fortunate because they patrolled an extremely large, busy district. From St. Louis Park's west border to Chicago Avenue and from Franklin to 32nd Street, they rode an unmarked squad and backed up three marked cars, taking their over-loads and going in on heavy stuff. When guns or knives or large groups in volatile situations were involved, Lapinsky and Giles were to move in auto-matically and they did.

It was a friendly district. People in the streets were always extending their hands to those in need. In need of having their purses snatched or their pock-ets picked, that is. Even hold up men had to keep an eye out for muggers or they'd be rolled on the way to their getaway cars.

These two officers were six footers in their mid-twenties. Each sported a full crop of dark hair. Each was college educated and each was a scholar when it came to criminal code books, police journals, sta-tistical crime reports, supreme court rulings and other law enforcement data. You name it, they knew it.

The frequency of striking similarities in squad team members always amazed me. It seemed as if they were matched up by some unseen designer who had a mania for keeping things in pairs. Perhaps those who made the matches were urged to consider similarities in make-up, I don't know. If they were, they did a good job of it. At any rate, these two men were definitely a pair.

The guys were so much into the law kick we referred to them as The Attorneys. In fact, we often thought of hanging a shingle in their squad: LAPINSKI and GILES, Attorneys at Law. Their names even sounded like those of law partners.

There were times their spouting off legalities wore a little thin but it eventually got them where they wanted to go. Lapinski now has an administrative job and Giles is in an investigative unit.

It wasn't unusual for patrolmen to find the attorneys discussing legalities while their "arrestees" stood around and waited for them to make up their minds. I was within earshot on one such occasion.

"OK, Lapinski," Giles said, "are we going to call this a 609.225, subdivision one or subdivision two?"

"Let's see, that's aggravated assault. It would be subdivision one obviously," Lapinski ruled. " 'Whoever intentionally inflicts great bodily harm upon another may be sentenced to imprisonment for not more than 10 years or to payment of a fine of not more than $10,000, or both.' "

"But the gun . . . ," Giles objected. " 'Whoever assaults another with a dangerous weapon but without intent to inflict great bodily harm may be sentenced to prison for not more than 5 years or to payment of not more than $5,000, or both.' "

"The gun is on the ground, remember?" Lapinski overruled. "This guy throws it on the ground before he attacks."

"Why does he throw the gun on the ground?" Giles asked, continuing his interrogation as though he had a 12-man jury which needed that point brought out.

The arrestee came to his own defense. "Because I don't want to accidentally shoot the guy," he said.

"Because he doesn't want to accidentally shoot the guy," Lapinski repeated.

"Well, that makes sense," Giles agreed. "Maybe it *is* a subdivision one then. But would you call a bloody lip and a broken nose 'great bodily harm?' "

"*I* wouldn't," the arrestee said, still representing himself. "Besides, I didn't intentionally inflict it."

Lapinski heard him that time. "Shut up or five will getcha ten," he said. Then he turned back to his law partner. "I think we should go for a 609.22— just regular assault. 'Intentionally inflicts or attempts to inflict bodily harm . . .' "

"I guess that's the proper way to go about it," Giles admitted. "Let's see, that's not more than 90 days or more than $100, or both."

"I can handle that," the self defender said hopefully.

Lapinski heard that, too. "Shut up or we'll get you on a 609.275," he growled.

"Which is?" the young man asked with genuine interest. By now he was *really* curious about the finer points of the law he'd broken.

"Attempt to coerce," Giles said obligingly.

"And that could get you up to 20 years," Lapinski added before he dismissed court.

"Geeze," the guy whispered under his breath before he shut up.

And that's the way it was with these two law book worms. I remember one night we went in on a drug raid without any warrants. I'd seen several dopers make a buy so I knew we had the goods on them, but there just wasn't time to go through the formality of getting a warrant for their arrests.

There were several of us and our main concern was getting the job done. We didn't knock, we just stormed in, searched the place for drugs and handcuffed everybody. And all the while, Lapinski and Giles just kept asking, "Is it legal? Are we within our rights? Is this according to the book?"

The attorneys were an exception when it came to wild parties, however. They *liked* to handle that detail, especially Lapinski, and they didn't waste time discussing rules.

"He's got a mad-on for parties," the chief said of Lapinski.

I saw him standing by his locker one Friday night before shift. He was wearing gloves and pounding a fist into the palm of his hand. "What's with the fingers?" I asked. "You think it's cold out there?" It was July.

"Here, feel 'em," he said, proudly extending his hand. "They're lined with fine metal BB's . . . almost like sand. Can't wait to clobber somebody with 'em."

"You'll have your chance," I said. "Tonight's party night."

"I know," he said enthusiastically, "and I'm ready for them."

We discussed our inability to understand the attraction of the booze bash. How could a hundred or more people actually enjoy jamming themselves into one room—with only about 2 square inches of breathing space apiece and no elbow room whatsoever—and drinking themselves blotto? And with the blaring racket from horrible stereos, how could they hear well enough to engage in any sort of conversation, or well enough to get into fights over something somebody said?

"I think perhaps because all human beings have an inherent need to express themselves to those individuals who can identify with their innermost feellings," Lapinski offered. "They need to experience the efficacy of acceptance; and failing to secure it from society, they assemble themselves with those of like mind."

"Oh," I said. "I always thought it was ennui."

He was surprised I knew an erudite term. "What do you mean by that?" he asked.

"Boredom," I answered simply.

"You could be right," he said and then he offered to do some extensive research on the subject. I told him to forget it.

I knew the kids needed something to give their lives meaning and they needed someone to minister to them about how Christ could give them that meaning. I knew if I told Lapinski and Giles they were supposed to be ministers, they'd say, "Yes, but is it legal?" And if I pointed out it says so in the Bible, they'd say, "Yes, but does it say so in the Minnesota Criminal Code?"

* * * * *

While some of the men I worked with agreed the prison systems were scarcely more than excellent crime schools and that locking up criminals fell woefully short of being an effective crime deterrent, they still felt it was the only choice they had. They could offer no suggestions for something better. Some of them, however, believed that government sponsored rehabilitation programs and prison reform efforts were the answer. And that was the thinking of many of the prominent voices in the country for a time. But such efforts have failed and now the pendulum is swinging to a get tougher policy.

In his book *Punishing Criminals*, Ernest Van Den Haag says, "The preservation of society and of the social order, finally, may require that we subordinate charity, and sometimes even justice, to punish most severely what most endangers society and the social order, even when there is little guilt, or none."

John R. Manson, Commissioner of Correction in Connecticut has this to say about rehabilitation efforts: "With only a few exceptions, there's no relationship to recidivism, no matter what the program."

Edmund G. Brown, Jr., Governor of California, states, "Prisons do one thing very well. They don't rehabilitate too well, but they punish pretty good . . . if you're going to prison we're not going to give you psychotherapy and psychologists and all that junk. I don't think that works. Prison is not pleasant—it's not supposed to be."

"Rehabilitation, whatever it means, and whatever the programs that allegedly give it meaning, must cease to be a purpose of the prison sanction." So says Norval Morris, Dean of the University of Chicago Law school.

"It requires not merely optimistic but heroic assumptions about the nature of man to lead one to suppose that a person, finally sentenced after [in most cases] many brushes with the law, and having devoted a good part of his youth and young adulthood to misbehavior of every sort, should, by either the solemnity of prison or the skillfulness of a counselor, come to see the error of his ways, and to experience a transformation of his character." That from *Thinking About Crime* by James Q. Wilson, professor of government at Harvard.

"The truth is, correctional administrators would be glad to rehabilitate all offenders if they only knew how. Society's illusion that they can is a result of the language that has surrounded corrections in recent years... gradually a medical model was created that implied offenders were sick, that we could diagnose their ailments as we do with people who are physically or mentally ill, and then prescribe a 'treatment' program which would bring about a cure," says Norman A. Carlson, director of the Federal Bureau of Prisons.

With this type of pessimism voiced by such prominent authorities, it isn't surprising the government is now leaning toward the get tough policy. But they are misinformed if they believe it's going to serve as a deterrent to crime. Many of them believe it will, however.

Former Attorney General William Saxbe declared, "If you catch people and you prosecute them, and you punish them, it is a deterrent to crime."

In his State of the Union Message, former President Gerald Ford stressed the deterrent value of imprisonment: "To keep a convicted criminal from committing more crimes, we must put him in prison so he cannot harm more law-abiding citizens. To be effective, this punishment must be swift and it must be certain."

Time Magazine reports that Senator Edward Kennedy, believing rehabilitation efforts have failed, has taken the position that punishment is society's best deterrent.

So some of the best minds in the country admit they don't have the answers, but incarceration is the only measure they can come up with.

I maintain getting tough won't work. Now, I'm not advocating the abolition of prisons. We must have them. And I'm not saying the policeman must be lenient. God commissions them to get tough if they have to as is pointed out in Romans 13. What I'm saying is that getting tough is not the permanent solution to the problem. Whether we've been lenient or whether we've been stringent, one fact stands out: crime has been and is rising at a rapid rate. Reported offenses classified mostly as major crime (i.e., criminal homicide, forcible rape, robbery, assault, burglary, larceny and auto theft) totaled 44,383 in 1975, even though 837 chiefs, deputies, inspectors, captains, lieutenants, sergeants and patrolmen were out there doing a job. Now I'm talking about Minneapolis alone.

Added to that figure should be the 196,408 miscellaneous services policemen rendered in 1975 in Minneapolis and one can see how monumental the individual cop's job is. (Those services include such things as investigating deaths, suicides, complaints, non-vehicular accidents and so forth.)

Now we have a total of 240,791 occasions which called for the services of a law officer. And that sum doesn't include traffic violations. That's another 333,003 for a new total of 573,794. Again, that's in Minneapolis alone and for just a 12-month period. And only God knows how many crimes went undetected and unreported. If that figure were added on, we can be assured it would be staggering. And if we properly multiplied it by every city in the country, we wouldn't believe the resultant sum. We couldn't believe it!

The crime rate in Minneapolis has tripled in a dozen years, as it has in most cities throughout the country; and there *are* cities in which the rate has climbed even higher—much higher.

Then why don't we triple the numbers in law enforcement and take care of the problem once and for all? And why don't we slap all the offenders behind bars and keep them there?

Well, for one thing, the taxpayers couldn't stand the load. States and counties now spend already more than $2.5 billion a year on new prisons at a cost of roughly $50,000 per cell. (Pretty expensive housing for those who disobey the laws of the land. Would that all law abiding citizens could live in homes of comparable value!) And that's just the tip of the iceberg when it comes to the expense of crime. But more importantly, additional staffing won't work because the traditional forms of law enforcement don't work!

The crime problem in this country is so vast and so serious it ought to scare the living daylights out of every citizen in it. And it's going to get worse. According to the annual statistical report issued by the Minneapolis police department in 1975, "A recent seven-county metropolitan area crime study reports that juveniles accounted for 61% of arrests for serious crimes and 40% of all arrests for crimes of violence. Although these statistics may vary from one jurisdiction to another, it can readily be seen that juveniles are involved in a major proportion of crime which plagues our society."

Our statistics compare with those of any city one cares to mention, so the next generation which will run this country will be made up in large numbers of well-trained criminals!

Hopefully they'll change their ways by then, comes the plaintive, blind cry of the misinformed who would push for conventional rehabilitation programs.

Oh no they won't! The study goes on to say, "Repeaters still make up the majority of contacts with 70.6% of those processed by officers of the division having had previous contacts with the police. And approximately 25% of those arrested were on parole or probation at the time of their arrest for a new offense!"

On CBS's nationally televised program, *60 Minutes,* Mike Wallace just about said it all when he stated, "Rehabilitation doesn't work. Nothing works."

Just about but not quite... because there's one thing that *will* work and that's the miracle of the changed life. I'm convinced that's the only permanent solution that exists and I've been in the business of law enforcement for ten years. I've seen the best plans of good men fail. And they fail because man, without God, cannot save his fellow man from sin. And crime *is* sin. He told us that 2,000 years ago and we've been too blind to see, too deaf to hear and too dumb to speak. We've ignored the greatest authority of them all, the Lord and Savior Jesus Christ, the Prince of Peace, whose methods cannot fail because He is the Son of God.

When I fully understood He has the approach to dealing with crime in the streets and that His commission to policemen is to use that approach, I made up my mind I would no longer be too dumb to speak out on the subject. I would tell every law enforcement officer who would listen because it's that law officer who, more than anyone else, is provided with the opportune moments, the crucial moments, in dealing with the sin-sick souls who break the laws of God and man.

But I had taken my in-depth look at the men around me and I was stumped as to how to get the message across.

Chapter XI

The Miracle

Most of my fellow officers were heavy into the police trip with a dedication that, while admirable, left scarcely any room for exploring other approaches to the serious problems they were asked to handle each day. The fact I was a Christian was of little concern to them save for their occasional interest in razzing me about it. I didn't mind that for they were generally good natured. I felt I had their respect; but of course, not being Christians themselves, they couldn't understand what motivated me.

"Lord, how do I witness?" I'd ask in prayer and it was as if He replied, "Wait." I didn't realize I was putting the cart before the horse ... that there was something else coming first ... something big ... that I would be involved in it and that the involvement was just around the corner. Luckily, I couldn't see around corners.

If I could have, I might have turned tail and run at the awesomeness of it all for I'd most likely have said, "Lord, I can't handle that job; it's too big."

But fortunately for me, God wisely took me a step at a time and showed me that if I trusted Him,

I could handle anything He gave me because I was merely an instrument through which He did His work. The battle was His. All I had to do was be willing to stand in the firing line and victory was assured.

There were two Christian men on the police force with whom I had contact, however, and they understood my frustrations in wanting to do something about my joint commission of being a cop for the city and a disciple for the Lord. One was Mike Oliveri, a good-looking Italian who started rookie school the same time I did and the other was Jim Robertson who worked in the planning and research department at City Hall.

Mike was interested in the work I had done with drug addicts at Teen Challenge in New York and he often asked me about it. Now and then he'd express an interest in doing something like that and one day he decided he would. "I want to take a year's leave of absence and work there," he said. "Think the chief will go for it?"

"Won't hurt to ask," I replied, not realizing the full implication of Mike's question.

"All right, I will," Mike continued, "but I'm going to need a back up unit when I go in there. Would you come with me when I talk to him tomorrow?"

"What about Robertson?" I asked, remembering tomorrow was my day off and that I was planning to stay home.

"He said he would. I want both of you."

Mike was serious. He'd already set the time and he'd already solicited Jim's help. I couldn't let him down. "Sure, I'll go," I said.

Thinking about it later made me jumpy. I didn't think the chief could possibly be interested in what I had to say. I didn't have much in the way of clout or seniority on the force and I wasn't so sure in my own mind that Mike's idea was a good one. But Mike seemed to think so and I had said I'd go with him. My job was to try to sell the idea to Gordon Johnson, Chief of Police, and I decided the thrust of my comments would be that Oliveri would return to the force a wiser and more effective cop—particularly in dealing with drug addicts.

The story of that meeting and what followed to get a mighty ball rolling is told in my book, *Miracle at City Hall*; for it was indeed a miracle and it marked the beginning of a whole new ministry—not only for Mike Oliveri but for me. I was given a project. One I'd never dreamed of ... not even in my wildest fantasies!

The project did not begin, however, with calling all the city cops together in one big room so that I could tell them about God's purpose for their lives. That purpose was to be revealed in another way, but much later, and *then* the "force" in law enforcement would be placed before the cart.

God had raised up one preacher cop, but I wasn't to be the only witness. There would be many others and there would be a program so all encompassing, so successful in rehabilitating devastated lives that law enforcement officers all over the world would look up to see the glory and the power of His mighty works. *Then* they'd understand the purpose of their roles. *Then* they'd catch the vision.

But I'm getting ahead of the story. There's no way to relate the entire content of *Miracle at City Hall* and it isn't necessary; but some of the salient points of that book bear repeating here in order that the reader comprehend the full significance of the Master's master plan and the thrilling, miraculous sequence of events that unfolded in the development of it.

Mike was granted his leave. Then Chief Johnson

turned his attention to me. "Don't you think we ought to have a program like Teen Challenge in Minneapolis, Palmquist?" he asked. "Maybe you ought to start one."

And the next thing I knew, I was walking with the chief into the office of Charles Stenvig, mayor of the city of Minneapolis! My heart was pounding and I wondered what he was going to say. I remembered a statement he'd made when he first took office: "God is my boss. I'll take my orders from Him," and I relaxed somewhat with the assurance that whatever it was, God had a hand in it.

The assignment was exactly what the Chief of Police had suggested: Set up a drug rehabilitation program in Minneapolis. "I've read several of Wilkerson's books," the mayor said, "and I'm convinced that any program without Christ is not the solution."

"How do you want me to put the thing together?" I asked, expecting an answer that would spell it all out in details I could understand.

"I'm the mayor; you're the preacher," he chuckled. "My only advice is no government grants. We don't want to push God out the back door."

In a sense, the mayor was saying to me what David Wilkerson had said a few years earlier. When I'd expected to enter some sort of training program before I dealt with drug addicts, Dave spelled out my instructions in one sentence: "Go out on the streets and trust the Lord."

My head spun then and it was spinning now.

The chief had one specific starting point for me as we left the mayor's office that day. "I'll have you transferred to juvenile division within two weeks," he said. "Meanwhile, start working on a plan and get yourself a board of directors."

I got to work.

First, I wanted the program to get the person free from drugs, true, but I didn't want it to stop there. We would help the addict to reenter society successfully. To do so we'd attack the problem from three areas of concentration: personal instruction, therapy and vocational guidance. When I finished my blue print, I realized the program would be patterned almost entirely after Teen Challenge. There would be one major difference, however. Midwest Challenge, the name I decided to call it, would eventually become self-supporting and that involved owning and operating a business.

It all looked so good on paper I was fairly lathered up with excitement when I read it and I could see the future looked bright. I'd finally be able to do something tangible in getting at the heart of problems I'd only been able to take pot shots at for so long. Instead of the frustration of locking up criminals and having them return to society better trained in crime, I'd know the satisfaction of being able to house them in facilities where I could help them, then teach them to go back into the world trained in the Word of God and in vocations that would make them useful, contributing members of society.

Not bad for starters. All I needed was a large house or two, a board of directors, a thriving business and a heap of money! Quite an order. But once I placed it, He filled it as per His promise: "But my God shall supply all your need according to His riches in glory." And since His riches exceed all our capacities to envision them, He supplied accordingly and brought far more than my limited mind could conceive. And the plan I had detailed was expanded to include areas I hadn't taken into consideration. There wasn't a concern I had had all through the years of frustrating work on the force that wasn't to be met. There wasn't a question that wasn't to be answered. There wasn't a prayer that was to go unheeded.

It was as if He said as He opened the floodgates, "So you want a board of directors, do you? Well, here's one comprising the cream of my crop. So you want a big house, do you? Well, here are two just for starters and I'll throw in a coffee house to boot. So you want a business, do you? Well, I've got a trusted servant who owns one and I'll have him give you a call one of these days. And remember your concern about helping people with domestic problems? Remember the dying, the wounded, the sorrowing? Well, I'll help you set up a drug program for addicts, but I'll take care of those others, too. I'll raise up a chaplaincy corps to deal with their problems. What's more, policemen themselves and their families could use understanding, counseling, bolstering. I'll see to it they get it. And all that is just the beginning. Money? No object. Ask and you shall receive."

When word got around juvenile what I was going to be doing, there were undercurrents of criticism that came to me from other officers in the division. One of the narcotics detectives was brazen enough to voice them. "I heard you're going to get drug addicts saved," he said in a condescending tone. "You're crazy. There's no way to help a drug addict."

Before I could tell him that I was merely the instrument and that God would do the saving, he strode off down the hall.

Before the drug program was to get underway, however, God was to get me working with His other program. I first became aware of it when Robertson called me to say a meeting had been arranged with Quint Alfors, director of the Greater Minneapolis Association of Evangelicals (GMAE), and two other men from his organization. They had come to Chief Johnson offering to provide a chaplaincy program which would handle such matters as domestic problems, death notices, suicide attempts and alcohol-related problems. Their plan was to offer help in the way of counseling and they'd provide their own car, radio, and other necessary equipment. They expected nothing in return for their services—only the opportunity to help. When they related their plan, I was amazed. It was all so simple. Why hadn't somebody thought of it before? When the men left, the chief turned to me. "Well, Palmquist," he asked, "what do you think of their idea?"

"I really dig it," I said with enthusiasm.

"Good," he replied, "because I want you to train them."

So two nights a week in the 6th precinct house on 26th and Nicollet, I held a mini-police academy for preachers. And the first thing I told them was, "I hope you guys are really right with the Lord because you just might be laying your lives on the line."

The acceptance of the Chaplaincy Corps by citizens and police officers was immediate. Their logs averaged three calls daily with domestics ranking highest on the list. A wide variety of other calls included everything from suicide attempts to death notices to counseling drunks.

A man who later became a member of the corps, John Owen, helped solidify a plan to include policemen and their families as part of the counseling program. He recognized that these forgotten members of society had needs that weren't being met.

He knew that police officers, seeing so many nega-
tive aspects of society, often become depressed and
that the depression rubs off on their families. They
need to unwind with someone they trust and their
wives and children need to air their apprehensions,
their fears and their frustrations. "I feel as though
a great load has been lifted from me," one of the
women said. "I'm so grateful to God He has arranged
this service for us."

To get the ball rolling on the drug rehabilitation
program, Mayor Stenvig sent a letter to all churches
in the Minneapolis area stating that drug abuse was
a growing problem and that he was convinced the
only solution was a program similar to Teen Challenge in New York City. He was, as he stated in
the letter, releasing Al Palmquist, a member of the
police department, to work on it. He solicited help
from these churches by asking them to set up speak-
ing engagements for me and to set aside what they
could financially for support of the program.

Quint Alfors suggested prominent members of
various churches who could serve on the board of
directors of Midwest Challenge; Jim Robertson also
suggested several people, and eventually we ended
up with a twelve-member board. Rev. Gordon K.
Peterson, pastor of Soul's Harbor Church in downtown Minneapolis, was one of them. He immediately
invited me to participate in four radio programs on
which he interviewed me about the proposed Midwest
Challenge and also gave me opportunity to give my
testimony. Later on, I appeared on two television
programs for Soul's Harbor. As a result of those
appearances and of the mayor's letter, churches began to make requests. The Lord took it from there
and we've been booked solid ever since.

When the *Minneapolis Star* and *Tribune* ran a

short article about the police department being involved in a drug rehabilitation program, two junkies
called up and wanted to get in. They'd seen the article, though it was buried way back toward the ad
section, and they wanted to know if the program
had started. That was real encouragement, not only
to me but to Chief Johnson. We'd both been getting
a bit nervous about the whole thing. As policemen,
we were beginning to have reservations that addicts
would be willing to trust us for help. We were definitely a class of people they avoided at all cost.

Their inquiry got us going with the request we'd
made for a house. I had contacted earlier a Christian
realtor who had been a friend of mine through the
years and he was scouting possibilities for me. But
I was fussy. I wanted a big house and though I had
looked at some 200 photographs of big houses and
had studied their floor plans, I had rejected them
all. I wanted something similar to the one Teen Challenge had in New York—one with a room in it big
enough to be used as a chapel. When I thought we'd
never find the right one, the realtor called to say
he thought he'd located the place I'd been looking
for. "Meet me at 3045 Columbus in an hour," he
said.

The house was then being used as a rest home
for mentally retarded women, but because of new
regulations, the owner was being forced to sell. The
home was anything but inviting—it needed a good
redecorating and a good airing out, but we visualized
the potential of it and decided this was it.

The owner, a stocky little red-headed Jewish woman, was asking $31,000 for the place completely fur-
nished. I offered $24,000 and she took me up on it.
We needed $6,000 for a down payment which seemed
a monumental sum . . . especially since we had the

grand total of $60 in our bank account!

But Harland Erickson, our treasurer-elect and vice president of Northwestern National Bank at Lake and Nicollet, agreed to stick his neck out and finance the deal.

As the months passed, money began to come in but we were still $2,000 short two weeks before the deadline. God met our need, however, and on March 31, 1972, I walked into the conference room at Northwestern National Bank, made the down payment of $6,000 and signed the papers.

In late June, Quint Alfors came to me to discuss a problem. GMAE operated a coffee house named Heavy Waters, its director had resigned and the place was closed. It was Quint's responsibility to find a new director.

"Good," I said. "I've been feeling God wanted us involved in that place."

I knew that with such a spot we'd have many more contacts and potential problem people for our program. It was a place that attracted many kids off the streets. Hearing music, they'd wander in, many of them high on drugs.

We decided the Midwest Challenge staff would operate it while GMAE would continue to support it financially. We redecorated, changed the name to LOGOS and reopened charging "50¢ admission if you have it." It's a place where the message of Christ is shared and where help is offered to those in need. Folk groups and Christian rock groups supply special music each night. Cookies, coffee and donuts are served throughout the evening.

The downstairs level has two small prayer rooms, a bookshop and a lounge where it isn't unusual to find someone sprawled out and spaced out on drugs. But counselors are aware of what goes on and they move throughout the crowd quietly sharing the message, as do others who have found Him there.

The miracles of changed lives surrounding that coffee house would fill a book in itself. One "hopeless" alcoholic wandered in one night, thinking it to be the bar down the street, and that marked the beginning of a new life for him. He is now an assistant foreman at Central Mailing Service, the business we bought with the purpose of becoming self-supporting. His story is matched by hundreds.

Shortly after we finished remodeling the center on Columbus Avenue and opened it for business, several girls came for help. Since the Health Department had said we could house only boys in the place, I sent up a prayer for help, knowing there is nothing chauvinistic about God. He, in turn, spoke to the heart of a minister's wife and she called me though she didn't know what for she said.

"You don't happen to have a house we could use, do you?" I asked, half wondering whether God had supplied the answer to my prayer and half expecting He had.

"That's it," she said delighted. "Yes, that's it. We *do* have a house. It used to be a parsonage, but now it's empty."

We received OK's from both the church board and the village council and a year after we opened the boys' home, we opened the home for delinquent female drug addicts at 7115 Fifth Avenue South.

About six months later I received a call from John Hartzell who employed ex addicts at a mailing service he managed. A devout Christian, John counseled the young people along with training them, and he wondered whether or not Midwest Challenge might be interested in buying the business so that it would have a means of supporting itself. Were we interested! I'll say.

God supplied the money for a small down payment

and what has happened since is again, miraculous. Young men and women are thoroughly grounded in the Word of God and are guided by Mr. Hartzell and others each day. A fine counselor and a creative man with ideas that never stop, he has also come up with a unique manufacturing operation which distributes products that tell the story of Christ. So Central Mailing now has a parent company, Ark Products, set up to handle the new phase of business. God turns out miracles by the minute down there.

And that's the story related in *Miracle at City Hall*, the story of a project God developed to answer the prayers of a preacher cop who found out He meant business when He said, "Ask and you shall receive."

But He didn't stop there. There's more.

Chapter XII

The Expansion

God had given us a corner on the block when we acquired that first house at 3045 Columbus. Little did we realize that within a year's time, He'd make six more houses on that street available and provide the means by which we could secure them. And later He'd add yet another two, one of them in a neighboring state, plus two more businesses, both offshoots from Central Mailing Company, our initial business enterprise.

I don't mean to imply it was all just that simple. It wasn't. Our first steps into the venture which resulted in the now broad, inclusive, Christ-centered drug rehabilitation program, were trembling ones but they were steps of faith. And God honored that faith. There were insurmountable obstacles along the way. He gave us wings to surmount them. We worked . . . hard. He gave us results. We prayed . . . constantly. He heard and He answered . . . always in ways that exceeded our limited conceptions of what we thought the answers would or should be.

Our adventure in faith was always exciting, however. The acquisition of the house on Chicago Avenue, for example.

It didn't take long before we outgrew the parsonage we were permitted to use for starting a girls' program. We needed more space for more girls who needed the program desperately.

On one particular day my concern for these young women led me to take a simple stroll around the block. I looked at each house wondering whether we could buy it, or rent it or use it somehow. Each seemed occupied. No lawns sported for sale signs. But the last house on my circuit—the second house from the corner on Chicago Avenue and directly behind the one we owned—looked deserted. A small sign in the window caught my eye and I walked up to get a closer look. I noted a federal organization called HUD was selling the place and that a phone number was listed.

I was excited. I dashed to the nearest phone and placed a call. "I'd like to buy that house," I said. "How do I go about it?"

"It will go to the highest offer by sealed bid," a voice answered.

"How can I be assured I'll make the highest offer?" I asked, feeling certain this house was meant for purchase by Midwest Challenge.

"You can't," came the answer. "You'll have to take your chances with the others. Put your bid in a sealed envelope and be at such and such a place . . ."

For the Christian who has learned to trust without doubt, this sort of challenge presents no problem. He is so sure of the matter being totally in God's hands, he doesn't worry about the outcome. He knows if God wants him to have the house, he'll have it. If he doesn't get it, he knows God has something better in mind.

It wasn't that easy for me. I worried, I wondered,

I stewed. I thought there would be hundreds of offers on that property. It was zoned for commercial as well as residential and many entrepreneurs would have an eye on it. And I knew all of them had more money than we did. We had exactly nothing. I called Harland Erickson, our banker board member. "What's the place worth?" I asked.

He and another banker named Chet Egan looked at the house. It was a large, well built 9-bedroom home in good condition. What with the attraction of commercial zoning, the men estimated its value at $30,000. I didn't bat an eyelid because I knew at that price it would be a good deal.

Even so it was out of reach. I wondered what to do when all of a sudden it occurred to me to claim a promise: " . . . if two of you shall agree on earth as touching any thing that they shall ask, it shall be done for them of my Father which is in heaven."

Just for good measure, I decided to double the stipulated number so I called three praying men together: John Hartzell of Central Mailing, Chuck Hetland who at that time was John's assistant and Chuck Shuler, a real estate agent who had taken a couple of years off from his business to lend his expertise to us in developing ours. And with myself, of course, we made a foursome.

I requested that each man ask God for a number. Then I called Harland and asked him to do the same. We added the figures and divided by five. Anybody with any financial acumen witnessing the strange business meeting would have told us we were crazy, but we had long since learned God's way of handling business is not always in accordance with man's logic.

The lowest amount given was $11,200—the highest

$13,000. The average came out to be $11,657.00 so we thanked God for supplying the figure, wrote it down on a piece of paper and sealed it in an envelope.

Then Chuck Shuler and I, with nothing in our hands but a slip of paper, but armed with the prayers of our companions, went to the auction. I confess I hoped our competitors had forgotten the time and place and wouldn't show up.

They appeared en masse! The large public room was so packed I couldn't believe there were that many people in Minneapolis with eyesight keen enough to have seen that small sign in the window. I grabbed my partner's arm. "Chuck," I whispered with trepidation, "we don't stand a chance. There are too many people here."

"Just wait," he said, his tone giving no indication of what his feelings were. I assumed he was curious to learn just who our new backyard neighbors would be.

Mocking doubts raced through my mind. How ridiculous of us to bid $11,000 for a $30,000 house and think we stood a chance! We wouldn't even be anywhere near the ball park. And even if we were, we didn't have a dime.

But I had momentarily forgotten just who had entered the bid. The truth was, it was ridiculous of me even to think of doubting the outcome!

Our bid was the highest ... and by just enough breathtaking dollars to make us rejoice all the more in the awesomeness of God!

But there was a hitch and it came as quite a blow. We were informed we couldn't finance the house in any way. We had to pay cash for it and we had just two weeks to come up with the entire amount.

There was only one thing to do. Ask. We knew

the God who had given us the bid would supply the money to make it good. I called my board together. We prayed, asking and expecting to receive. I then drafted a news letter which we sent to the some 7,000 people we had on our mailing list at that time and within two weeks, the money was there!

* * * * *

The way we were able to acquire a foster home for young teenage boys which is managed by Gene and Linda Francis is another example of the miraculous power of God ... of His perfect timing ... of His divine guidance and love.

When the owner of the home died, his son placed it on the market. As soon as the for sale sign was erected, we made haste to check on the details. The location was perfect. We needed the place. We wanted it.

The man was asking $17,000 and seemed eager to sell since he neither needed nor wanted the home. We offered $15,000 and to our surprise, he turned us down. We felt confident we could come to terms, but six months passed and nothing happened. We were disappointed but then, "Perhaps God is reserving it for us at $15,000," we thought.

Then it happened. Disaster struck. The sort of act of God one reads about in the fine print of insurance policies and subsequently discovers he isn't covered even though he could have sworn he was.

It was mid-winter. Minnesota winters can be bad ones and this one was. Sub-zero weather for days on end tested the endurance of the heating systems throughout the city as well as the stamina of its residents. Valiantly they bundled up and shoveled and shivered and plowed and thawed out everything that kept freezing up.

The strain was too much for the unattended furnace of the house on Columbus Avenue, however. It burst as well as did the pipes throughout the entire plumbing system. Water poured out everywhere, warping floors, ruining carpets and, in general, making a mess of the place.

It was then the owner paid us a visit. "You can have the home for what payments are left on it," he said, "and that's just a shade over $8,000."

Not wanting to be stuck with a pig in a poke, we had it appraised and found that its worth—damages and all—was $17,900. Obviously the owner had made us an extremely good offer. We bought. After putting in $6,000 in repairs, the house was appraised at $32,000—$18,000 more than our total investment!

* * * * *

Miracles like that happened every time we expanded. Not only was money provided but services were donated that saved us thousands upon thousands of dollars. Like the time we needed funds for electrical and plumbing work on still another house, for instance. I mulled the matter over in my mind one night—tossed and turned would be a better way of saying it—and at midnight my phone rang.

"Just felt prompted to call," a man said. "I hear you need money to hire some work done."

When I affirmed he had heard correctly, he said, "Don't worry about it. I'll do the whole job for nothing."

I gulped and momentarily wondered whether or not I'd been dreaming. But I was wide awake. I had heard correctly and in essence what the man had just said to me was, "I'll give you $10,000."

* * * * *

Midwest Challenge is the only effective Christian

drug rehabilitation center in a six-state area which includes Minnesota, North and South Dakota, Wisconsin, Iowa and Nebraska. Statistics acquired by Minnesota reveal that 20% of its population is chemically dependent on drugs. That means one of every five people is either drinking too much, popping too many pills or shooting too much heroin. Such figures indicate why workable programs such as ours must expand. Now God is moving us into Wisconsin.

We've just begun a branch program in Milwaukee which came about as the result of determination and persistence on the part of a Christian couple who wouldn't take "Let's wait and see" for an answer.

It all started when I spoke at a Women's Aglow meeting in Milwaukee. Afterwards, one of the members came up to me, handed me her phone number and said, "I must talk to you. Please call me tomorrow. It's urgent."

I said I would and fully intended to do so, but somehow or other I lost the number and couldn't make the call. I hoped she'd contact me again.

And she did . . . the very next night. I spoke at a Full Gospel Businessmen's meeting and afterwards both she and her husband came up. Again she asked that I call on an urgent matter, and again she gave me her number. Again I promised I would call.

Now I'm consistent, I'll say that for myself. Again I lost the number.

Two months passed. She called long distance. "I'm coming to Minneapolis," she said. "I just *have* to have an appointment with you to talk about an urgent matter!"

We set the time and place and I marked it on my calendar in large letters. By now, I was more than moderately curious to learn what the urgent matter was and I knew if I forgot the woman one

more time, I might never find out. I determined nothing save an act of God would keep me from that
appointment.

I was in Duluth, Minnesota the night the big snow
hit.

Waiting at the airport for the plane I was to board,
I learned that all planes were grounded and that
the one that was to take me back to Minneapolis
in time for my appointment was still in Denver.

Fortunately, the woman with the mysterious urgent matter to discuss was not the type to be stood
up, act of God or no. She determined to wait me
out no matter how long it took.

"My husband and I feel God has called us to start
a Teen Challenge in Milwaukee," she said without
preliminaries when we finally got together. "Can you
help us?"

"Don't do that," I told her. "Work for us and
we'll start a branch center out there." And as soon
as I said it I wondered why.

She left brimming with excitement and I don't
know how I could have forgotten the matter, but
I did. Until she called two months later.

"We've found the house," she said matter-of-factly. "Can you come out to look at it?"

So I went to Milwaukee. It was a beautiful home.
And it was in superior condition. There were 18 rooms
in all. The asking price was $31,000 and I knew it
was well worth that and more. Trouble is, we naturally didn't have any money, so I told the woman
we'd think about it and I flew back to Minneapolis
only to put the matter out of mind again.

But when she called once more to say she and
her husband had moved in, I decided the time had
come to call my board together and tell them the
whole story.

The home was divided into three separate apartments, each occupying an entire floor. The top floor was already rented out. Jim and Sue rented the second floor, and that left the third apartment vacant.

After some discussion of what our plans were, the owner of the home agreed we could tie up the property for one year for the unbelievable sum of $200. So that's what we did and we're now in the process of raising funds for the down payment.

Shortly after making the arrangement, however, something happened that shook us all up and blackened the name of Midwest Challenge. The police raided the third floor. Unknown to us, several dopers lived there and the officers had had their eye on them for some time. They naturally assumed we were part and parcel of the whole operation, so the news media picked it up and spread the word.

When the truth came out, however, they published a retraction to set things straight and our name was cleared. Even so, it was an earth-shaking experience.

Among those arrested were a man and wife who left a small child behind so our managers took him under their wings. At 2 1/2, the boy was well on his way to becoming an addict. His craving for drugs was insatiable and he knew all the ways to get the stuff into his system. Sue told me she first realized it when, going into the third floor apartment, she saw him pick up butts of marijuana cigarettes and draw on them like a pro. But when she told me he was also into cocaine, I couldn't believe it. I'd seen many young drug users in my day, but none under 10 or 12.

Cocaine can be used in different ways. One is to snort it—that's inhaling it through the nose. The sophisticated snorters—if one can call them that—use cocaine spoons made for the purpose. The un-

sophisticated use straws which work equally well.
"Whenever Joey sees a straw, he puts it to his nose
and inhales," Sue told me.

Still I had my doubts. But when I flew out there
shortly after things broke, I saw for myself. The
child scrambled across the breakfast table when he
saw my bottle of vitamin tablets, and screaming,
"Pills, pills," made a lunge for the bottle, upsetting
everything in his path. Obviously he thought they
were barbituates and he wanted them. When I was
told he slept far more than the average child his age,
I suspected he had been on seconal.

One thought hit home then and there. We must
make our program so inclusive we get to the young
kids. If we don't reach this fertile field now, those
who are ten or so will be addicts by the time they're
15. We've got to be preventative as well as curative.
That's the only way we can stamp out this horren-
dous problem once and for all.

There must be hundreds of children like Joey . . .
babies and toddlers of addicted parents who liberally
share drugs with their children . . . not out of gen-
erosity, but out of selfishness . . . to keep them quiet
or out of the way while they go about the insidious
process of destroying their bodies and minds. We
must prevent this waste, the saddest pollution of all—
the destruction of the human body and soul.

God knew the urgency of Joey's situation and sent
a determined woman and her husband to his aid
just in the nick of time. That incident alone convinced
me it was no accident this devout couple had literally
taken matters into their own hands and moved in
without the time it would have taken for our consent.
God had most certainly intended that we start the
branch center in Milwaukee and we have no doubt
He will provide the means for the down payment

on the home when the time comes.

* * * * *

We often wondered why we were making payments on every house we owned except for the one on Chicago Avenue. God had made a cash deal on that one. We understood why when it became apparent we needed a place to conduct our own Sunday services. Many—perhaps most—of our young people are turned off by the traditional forms of church worship and nothing or no one can convince them to attend services on Sunday. Perhaps they feel bitter ... perhaps they feel the traditional church has failed them and in a large sense, it has. But the thought of getting together themselves appealed to them and they said if they could have a church of their own they'd come regularly.

But for all our houses, we had no one house with a room big enough to accommodate all those who wanted to come. We needed our own chapel.

"Why don't we build one?" a young man in the program asked. His suggestion was a good one but it wasn't all that simple I pointed out. There was a matter of money.

"Well then, why don't we borrow it?" he asked, pursuing the matter.

"A person's got to have collateral for borrowing money to build," I explained. And then it occurred to me we owned one house lock, stock and barrel. Why not use that for collateral?

We got estimates of how much it would cost to build a modest structure, yet one large enough to accommodate our needs, and found that $25,000 would do it. We broached the subject to the banker who loaned us $22,000 just like that. We've just finished construction and the enthusiasm of the young people who are now using the new meeting room and chapel keeps growing daily.

* * * * *

So much for the acquisition of buildings ... of structures. The important thing is that they house living temples of His Holy Spirit, human lives. While the structures testify to God's glory, the buildings not made of hands testify of the mighty power of His salvation. These lives are proof that Jesus Christ does work miracles ... that He does change lives ... that He does heal the sick ... that He does forgive sin ... and that He does place within hearts a new spirit bringing joy and victory in all things.

Let me tell you about some of those living miracles.

Chapter XIII

Changed Lives

His case was hopeless. He'd blown his mind. One too many trips on LSD. Once the thinking part of the brain is reduced to such a state, there's no reversal. So the doctors at the hospital said.

It was a shame, too. Michael Muhar hadn't intended for things to be like that. All he'd wanted was to see what it was like. All he'd ever planned was to try it once. Just once. He wasn't going to get so strung out on the stuff he couldn't function or anything like that.

The trip was better than he'd imagined. Wow! What a way to take the hum drum out of the rat race! And it hadn't hurt him a bit. He'd come down OK, hadn't he? All that talk about LSD being so bad. Shucks, that's all it was ... talk. Well ... maybe it *did* hit some guys hard, but not good old Mike. The stuff worked for him. He was one of the lucky ones. He could take a trip every now and then. Or so he thought ... when he still had the capacity to think, that is.

But now Michael Muhar was a near basket case. They bounced him from one hospital to another like a steel marble in a pin ball machine; and after the fourth, they locked him up in a ward at the State Hospital. "This is going to be your home for awhile," they told him and Mike with child-like curiosity asked why.

There were three reasons they said. One, he had brain damage. Two, he had the mental capacity of an idiot. Three, if he were ever able to leave the hospital, he could never function in society. All he'd be able to do was put round pegs in round holes.

And while Michael Muhar didn't remember it, he'd heard that song before. All the doctors and all the shrinks at all the hospitals had told him that. And they weren't quacks either. They were top men in the fields of medicine and psychiatry. They knew whereof they spoke.

No one who's come to Midwest Challenge has been in worse shape than Mike. I don't know how he made it to us, but he did. He stuttered so bad it took me half an hour to find out his name. What happened after that can best be told by Mike:

"Al Palmquist didn't buy the doctors' prognoses. He didn't tell me I'd blown my mind. He didn't say I was an idiot. What he told me was that my relationship with the Lord wasn't right and if I'd get that straightened around, I could have a brand new life.

"While I found his comments encouraging, I had my doubts as to their validity. I'd been pegged as an idiot and I just kept on acting like one... a spoiled one to boot. Al didn't buy that either. Once when I was doing my number, he said, "Mike, when my three-year old acts like that I spank him."

"I was cocky enough to say, 'You wouldn't dare.' That's all it took to rile the big Irishman. He glared at me with those stern blue eyes of his and said, 'Mike, I'm a cop. I don't know how to go into all that counseling stuff you're used to and I don't take that kind of guff from anybody.' With that he stood up, came right over the top of his desk, grabbed me by the nape of my neck and beat the tar out of me.

"It's the best thing he could have done. He certainly got my attention and I started to listen. I respected him, too. It wasn't long after that I turned my life over to Christ and became the new man I'd been told I could be. My mind and my body were restored and I've been totally free of drugs ever since. What's more, I'm happy . . . happier than I've ever been in my life."

That was five years ago and today Mike works as an accountant for one of the major bookstore chains in Minneapolis. He'll tell anybody who will listen about the miracle that happened to him. This young man is living proof that with God, all things are possible.

* * * * *

The rich, full strains of lyrical beauty fill the auditorium as the young woman strums her guitar and sings, "I'll be home . . . when your life's in trouble and you're all alone . . . I'll be there to comfort you and see you through . . . " And there's something about her . . . and the way she sings that testify with quiet power to the absolute conviction that every word is true. And when she finishes, the room is so quiet you can hear a pin drop. The audience is moved.

Then Georgene Daubanton speaks softly. "Jesus is here tonight . . . He's in our hearts . . . He's feeling what you're feeling and He's loving you . . . whether you're down and out or on cloud nine . . . He's loving you . . . "

And the voice is so beautiful you can hardly keep

from crying and the singing is so very, very professional, you wonder under which great masters she's studied. You ask and you find that the master is Jesus. He put the song in her heart. She's had no formal training at all.

Georgene was a professing Christian before she came to Midwest Challenge and she came as one of our house parents. The scoffers and the skeptics who knew her background said we took her in because she was one of the more choice women of the streets. She'd run away from home as a teenager and had gotten heavily involved in the drug culture in California. She'd been in and out of jail. She was hard and she was bitter. She'd messed up her life and she hated herself. She went back home. One night her mother encouraged her to go with her to hear a preacher cop speak. Well, she'd had enough of cops and she'd heard enough preacher talk to last her a lifetime; but just to get her mother off her back, she acquiesced. She went to the meeting.

That was the start of a new life for Georgene. She renewed her faith, left the drug scene for the God scene and has been singing her story ever since. At the request of those who have heard her voice, Midwest Challenge has recorded albums of her music and these are becoming favorites of many who love inspirational music.

* * * * *

Imagine a speed freak—a cubehead, a pillhead, a pothead—teaching a bunch of cops how to elude a bunch of cops!

Steven Forsyth had an expensive habit to support and he couldn't do it on his salary even though it was a comfortable one for a kid 21 years old. So to augment his income he did a little moonlighting as a pusher—and he did it right on the job. He was cagey. He never once got caught by the cops. And he lived so high on drugs he nearly killed himself.

Steve was a model son, a model student, a model boy scout, a model everything. He believed in Mom and Dad, in God, in democracy, in school spirit and all those good things many modern young people view as just so much hypocritical poppycock.

He believed in his ideals so strongly, he began to wonder why life was so hard for so many people. They worked and saved and never got anywhere. He began to doubt that for all his idealism there was any pay-off at all. Then too, he had epilepsy and it finally occurred to him to blame God for it. It just wasn't fair to hang a rap like that on him. After all, he was such a good kid. Why, he'd even gotten to be an Eagle Scout and you've got to keep yourself physically strong, mentally awake and morally straight to do that. Didn't that mean anything to God? Especially the morally straight part?

Apparently not. And so, at the age of 16, Steve began to experiment with drugs. First he upped his medication, then he went for broke. He tried pot, LSD, mescaline, speed, barbituates, MDA and smack (heroin). By the time he was 21, he'd been in five centers for drug addiction. The third place released him with five prescriptions for drugs to get him off drugs. Somehow that didn't add up. He decided to opt for suicide.

Oh, he'd tried it before but always when his parents or his girlfriend were around so they could rush him in for help. He hadn't really wanted to die. But this time he was serious. He plotted his own cold-blooded murder. He secluded himself so that he wouldn't be found until it was all over and swallowed 2 1/2 bottles of barbituates. He slipped into a coma.

By all human reasoning he should have died but

he didn't. Three days later his young brother found him and asked simply, "Steve, do you *really* want help?"

Steve decided then and there he really did but his compulsion was so strong he was afraid he couldn't stick by the decision. So his parents took him to a fourth center in the Minneapolis area where he actually cried out asking God to prove His existence and help him. "Something started to happen after that," Steve says, "but I didn't know what at the time. When I was released from there, I was sent to a half way house in Minneapolis because they didn't want me back around my old friends in Viola. While at the new place I wandered down Lake Street one night and wound up in the Logos Coffee House. This guy named Tony sat down by me and we struck up a conversation. I told him the fix I was in."

"Your real problem isn't drugs," Tony said. "Your real problem is that you're living apart from the Lord. You need to quit running your own show and let Him take over your life."

And right then and there Steve asked the Lord to take charge of his life. He subsequently entered the program at Midwest Challenge and found what Tony had told him was true. He claimed freedom in Christ and gained freedom from drugs. It happened just like that. He was also cured of his epilepsy. He'd had grand mal seizures so frequently he was up to 600 milligrams of dilantin a day and still they wouldn't be controlled. He finally quit blaming his creator, accepted his malady and even praised God for it. He hasn't had a seizure in two years now and he doesn't take his medicine any more. We've had him checked by his doctors and they're baffled. His EEG tests have shown no trace that a problem ever existed.

Steve is one of the most dynamic young men in the program. He's especially effective as a leader of a kids' club we have and he's led many of these youngsters to Christ. He believes as I do, that if we don't get them now, they'll be junkies within three years.

Steve married the cook who prepared the first meal he ate at the center and the two of them are happy in living for the Lord.

In lending his ill-gotten know-how to interested cops by teaching a mini course in how junkies evade the law, Steve hopes to help them in cracking down on pushers and on burglaries which are a major concern in The Cities. Over 10,000 such crimes are committed each year and statistics indicate some 80% of them are committed by drug addicts who steal to support their habit.

*   *   *   *   *

Karen Durham had physical problems that raised such havoc with her emotions she began taking sleeping pills to get some rest at night. That was when she was a junior in high school. But she needed more than sleep. She needed to relax days, too. So she got a tranquilizer to calm her down... then another to lift her up... and finally she was on to six different kinds. Some would think that should have done it, but Karen needed more. She wanted to get off the see-saw... or get it to level out at least. She got a prescription for a seventh, then an eighth... and by the time she entered Midwest Challenge at age 23, she had 15 different prescriptions for tranquilizers and she was taking all of them! If there were a real Karen Durham housed in that trim body of hers, Karen didn't know who she was. Needless to say, she couldn't work. She'd never had a job in her life. Truly she was a pathetic case.

Certainly she deserved sympathy. Surely she'd have to go off her drugs slowly. Imagine her surprise when Dick Hardin, one of our staff workers, told her she had to quit cold turkey.

"I was scared," Karen says. "I was terribly, terribly scared. I didn't think I could do it. And when I tried, my emotions ran wild. I was shaky. I was nervous. I cried. In fact, I cried all the time."

We helped pray that girl through and she made it. She takes no pills at all now and she's working full time as a secretary in one of the offices at the University of Minnesota.

But that isn't all there is to the story. By the time Karen came to us, she'd been in six different hospitals and one half way house. She was diagnosed as a paranoid schizophrenic and she was deathly afraid of people. She was, to put it mildly, a hopeless case.

There's nothing schizoid about Karen today. She's a radiant Christian girl who trusts her Lord for everything. And she's got reason to shout it from the housetops ... not only for her release from drugs but for a dramatic healing of her physical condition.

Karen had a severe curvature of the spine. She hated her deformity. She tried to dress so that it wouldn't show. She naturally thought she'd have to live with it the rest of her life.

"But one morning I went to a church where Al Palmquist had been asked to speak. He talked about healing," she relates. "I don't remember too much of what he said. I was a fairly new Christian at the time and I really didn't understand much about it. But I sat there quietly and I said, 'God, if you really do such things, then show me. Just show me. Heal my back.'

"Well, my bones started cracking and my spine began to straighten and I walked out of that church a new woman!"

Talk about a miracle!

Karen frequently had severe earaches and sore throats also. She doesn't any more. "I claimed God's healing for those, too," she says.

For the paranoid schizophrenic, the drugged zombie-like girl who was so afraid of people she shuddered at the thought of being around them, it took great courage to break away from the old patterns. Karen knows God supplied that courage because she didn't have any of her own. He gave her the courage to go to business school to study secretarial skills. He gave her the courage to apply for a job. He gave her the courage to try again when she was fired from her first one. Oh, she cried about that, naturally. I told her not to give up, that God had a better job in mind for her. She believed it and not long after that, she got the position she now holds. She's been there over a year and she loves it. What's more, she's a capable, efficient employee.

* * * * *

Greg Sage rolled up a sleeve which covered the ugly, tell-tale tracks and pushed the jack into his arm. He drew blood and knew he'd hit the vein. Then slowly, with the skill of a well trained medic, he pushed the plunger in again, this time to inject the liquid that would get him off and up where he wanted to go. Greg had mixed this stuff himself. He'd ground up his amphetamines and dissolved them in water. Sure he could have popped his speed, but you get off faster if you shoot it.

He hadn't eaten in a week. His body was so full of liquid from shooting drugs, he didn't know how

it could take any more. It couldn't. Immediately
his chapped lips split open and the blood spurted
forth. Messy. But then, that's one of the hazards
of this business. It's awful. Deadly. Once a guy's
hooked, though, what's he gonna do? What choice
has he got? What hope?

Greg Sage started stealing from stores when he
was in the seventh grade and was put on probation
for it. Hardly worth it he thought, so he started selling
amphetamines instead. And he started upping his
own dosage. By the time he was in 9th grade he
had quite a reputation as a good supplier. He also
had a habit he couldn't kick. When he was in the
10th grade he was busted for selling the stuff. No
choice now, with a growing habit, but to go back
to stealing again. He staged a robbery. He was
caught . . . just a mile down the road. What a lousy
break! Since he was a juvenile, they sent him up
for 0-5 years at the state reformatory in St. Cloud,
Minnesota. What a lousy, stinking break!

But then he *did* get away from home. All that
fussing and arguing all the time was making his
life miserable anyway. All the fighting. He could
do without it . . . maybe. At least he was getting
even by causing his folks so much trouble and all.

By the time of his conviction, Greg had been in
and out of four different drug treatment centers. They
hadn't helped. He, too, was given drugs to get off
drugs. He, too, was diagnosed as a paranoid schizophrenic. He, too, was told all the things he already
knew: he was confused, he wasn't facing reality,
he wasn't accepting responsibility, he was power-
less over drugs.

But what hope was there? They didn't seem to
have any to give him.

So now he sat in a reform school. Well, he'd

reform if he knew how. But if all the doctors and all the psychiatrists at all those institutions couldn't tell him how to reform, how was this place going to do it? He didn't know.

But God did.

His mother came to see him.

"That was a miracle," Greg says, "the very fact she came to see me. She'd wanted nothing more to do with her son. But she'd been given a newsletter sent out by Midwest Challenge and somewhere along the line she'd been saved. She brought the newsletter and an application. She told me I could be paroled if I entered a drug program and this looked like a good one to her. But I'd have to write the letter myself. I'd have to initiate the action.

"I was leery of going any place run by a cop, and I certainly didn't want to correspond with one. The thought of begging one to take me in and help me made me cringe. Besides, all those other treatment centers hadn't helped. How could this one? Well, they *did* have a new gimmick . . . they talked about God. Then, too, I *did* want to get out on parole. I wrote the letter."

As is the case of many others, the end of Greg's story is the beginning of a new life for him. He came to Midwest Challenge and found his hope in Jesus Christ. He became a Christian and was healed of his addiction. His severe bouts with depression were prayed away and he's sharing the message of hope with others who have lost their way in the drug scene. At the time of this writing, Greg has spent 13 months at the Center and will be off probation in 30 days. His parole officers are pleased with the change they've seen in his life and they believe, at long last, that this kid is finally going to make it.

Of course he is. God doesn't run half way houses. He goes *all* the way!

* * * * *

Every word of every account related in this chapter is true. And these are but five of the scores of young people whose lives have been miraculously changed.

There are 200,000 drug abusers in the metropolitan Twin Cities area. Each addict spends from $50 to $500 a day to support his habit, and most derive their money from criminal activities which cost private citizens billions of dollars each year. Each one who is jailed costs taxpayers over $100 a day. It costs from $150 to $200 per day for each one who is hospitalized, yet the largest federal hospital in the country states that its cure rate is under 5%!

Our costs at Midwest Challenge are $13.50 per individual per day and our cure rate is an incredible 93.4%!

Can there be any doubt as to the abilities of the Great Physician? Is it any wonder that with statistics like these, people are getting the message? That law officers in Minneapolis and surrounding areas are no longer debunking the Christ-centered drug rehabilitation program? That they're saying there *is* something to it after all?

Some of them are beginning to do something about it.

Chapter XIV

The God Squad

If you're wheeling down the highway *modulating* with your *seat cover* and doing *double nickles,* things are probably cool. But *hammer down* and you might find a *bubble gum machine* in your rear view ... or possibly a *plain blue wrapper.* In which case you'll have to answer to the *Smokey* on your tail and that could cost you a bundle of green stamps or maybe a hitch in the pokey.

The lingo is CB slang for *talking, girl friend, 55 mph, accelerate, red lights, unmarked squad* and *cop.* The Citizens Band has developed an entire new vocabulary for jaw jacking—that's modulating— and it's catching on all over the country.

Down through the years cops have been called everything from Flatfeet to Fuzz to Pigs. We don't mind the new handle—Smokey—because the connotations are somewhat more complimentary. Smokey Bear is one well respected figure even though he is legendary. He's done a super job in getting campers and hikers to obey the laws of common sense.

There's a whole new breed of Smokies who,

having witnessed the miracles of changed lives in former trouble makers and drug addicts, have caught the gist of Romans 13 and are serving the Lord as ministers. We've given them a new handle: Holy Smokies.

Find yourself doing over double nickles in Appleton, Wisconsin, and you'll find the God Squad on your tail. In which case, you'd better brace yourself because you just might get it with both barrels— the Word of God, that is.

It all started when Officer Mike Phillips happened to read a copy of Hal Lindsey's *The Late Great Planet Earth*. He'd been to many churches in his day, but he'd never heard about such things as salvation or the rapture or the tribulation or the second coming. "If this stuff is true," he thought, "I'm in for a treat . . . provided I'm headed the right direction, that is."

Mike's the kind of cop who wants to know when there's trouble brewing. He's also the kind of cop who wants plenty of evidence on which to build a case. The tribulation sounded like big trouble to him . . . the kind citizens in his district ought to be warned about. But he wanted more evidence before he worded it around so he did some more research on the subject. He read Salem Kirban's *Guide to Survival*. Then he checked things out with the Bible. He found some 320 Old Testament prophesies had come to pass so he figured the New Testament prophesies weren't just so much pious prattle. That clinched it. Mike became a Christian.

Later he attended a Full Gospel Business Men's meeting, led by the director of Appleton's chapter, Dave Bruning, and it was there he dedicated his life to service. After that he couldn't keep his mouth shut about the Lord. He began to witness to the

men on his shift and one by one, like well-placed
dominoes, they fell in line for the Lord.

The first was Bill Stewart. Bill confided family
problems to Mike who asked if he'd ever prayed
about them. Bill hadn't thought of that so Mike asked
if he could pray for him right then and there. The
next day a surprised and happy Bill Stewart said,
"What are you in to anyway? That stuff really
works. When I got home last night my wife had
prepared the best meal she'd fixed in 5 years!"

Mike told him what he was "in to," continued
to witness to him, and within the year, Bill became
a Christian.

Bill then shared his experiences with Officer
Don Van Stipend and eventually he too accepted
Christ.

Mike then witnessed to Bill Linebach on coffee
breaks, which they sometimes took on the late shift
at the quietest spot they knew—the cemetery. Mike
wound up giving him a copy of *The Late Great
Planet Earth*.

Linebach, at that time, was taking police science
courses at the Fox Valley Technical Institute and
had been given an assignment to deliver a persua-
sive speech. Since *Planet Earth* presented the most
convincing agruments he'd ever heard of, Linebach
decided to give his speech on that. To do so, of course,
he had to take the stand of a Christian so that he
could refute the arguments presented by the class.
That did it. Linebach's speech was convincing all
right. He convinced himself to play the part for
real and later became a follower of the Lord.

Officer Les Trevor was already a Christian but
he was lukewarm about it and rarely made any
waves that would have indicated where he stood.
In Mike's pre-Christian days, Trevor had tried,

half heartedly, to get Mike to go with him to church; but when Mike said, "If I need that stuff I'll let you know," Trevor let the matter drop.

Now an enthusiastic Mike was trying to get Trevor to go with him to a Full Gospel Business Men's meeting and it was Trevor who was saying, "When I need that stuff, I'll let *you* know." But Trevor had witnessed a change in Mike Phillips and had noticed a happiness about him that wasn't there before. Besides, Mike was persistent so Trevor finally said he'd go to the meeting. It was there he re-affirmed his faith and that was the turning point in *his* life.

Now all the men—Phillips, Stewart, Von Stipend, Linebach and Trevor—began to witness to their supervisor, Lieutenant Bob Frayling.

The five religious freaks drove Frayling up a wall and he used four-letter words to express his irritation. When that failed, he used four-letter words to drive *them* up a wall and it frustrated him no end that he couldn't get the job done. It also surprised him. The men countered by placing Bible tracts everywhere... in Frayling's hat, in his squad, on his desk, in his pigeon hole. They also carried tapes of Christian music and Bible instruction and listened to them frequently. To which Frayling did things like kick wastebaskets down the hall. He also swore and he kept on swearing.

One day Von Stipend delivered a short sermon to his supervisor using as his text the scripture in James which speaks of the tongue as being the rudder of the ship and of the impossibility of salt water and fresh water coming from the same spring. Frayling got the gist and was irritated all the more. He thought these crazy tract packers and tape toters were up to some unique sort of con game and he vowed to find out what it was. And so, when the men invited him to join them one night for a prayer meeting, Bob Frayling accompanied them and he was all primed to spring like a fox when the time came for cracking the ring.

He sat rigid in the pew, his arms folded tight across his chest. Without the slightest movement of his head, he shot wary glances every direction except backwards. But his ears were tuned for the sound of any trouble behind him. No doubt about it, he was wired to explode and his fuse was short.

As the meeting progressed, however, the lieutenant began to relax and after about an hour he interrupted the session. "I may be out of order," he said to the group, "but I'd like to say something. I came here tonight because I thought my officers were up to some sort of con game and I intended to break it up. But I can see you people are sincere in your worship. I don't know what it is you've got, but whatever it is, I want it."

And that night Lieutenant Bob Frayling accepted Christ as the supervisor of his life and became one of the Holy Smokies on the God Squad.

With single mind these six outstanding men are serving the citizens of Appleton, Wisconsin in ways that make even doubting Thomases believers. They have started a fund which they use for purchasing tracts, Bibles and other inspirational literature; and when they go in on domestics or other cases involving people with desperate problems, they go in armed with the Word.

And they'll take calls whether they're on duty or not. Mike got out of bed one night when Linebach wanted help. "I've got a fellow down here who wants to commit suicide," he said, "and I don't think I can get through to him."

"I'll be there in fifteen minutes," Mike said and he made it in ten.

The man was 22 years old, had slashed his wrists—not just on that occasion but a few times before—and was adamant about not wanting to live. He'd been in and out of health centers, on and off tranquilizers and he couldn't shake the habit which, though purported to make his life a heaven on earth, made it an intolerable hell.

"Have you been living your life the way *you* want?" Mike asked him.

"Yeah," the man said. "I guess I'd have to say that."

"Has it got you anywhere?"

"No," the man admitted. "It's made me miserable."

"Got any idea what's wrong with you?" Mike asked, knowing full well what the problem was.

"Well, they told me at the center that I was psychotic ... that I had a whole bunch of things with names I didn't understand."

Using scripture, Mike went on to show him that man had had the same problems 2,000 years ago but then it was identified for what it is. "Your trouble," he told the young man, "is that Satan is attacking you and he's winning."

"I don't believe in Satan," the man replied, "*or* God for that matter."

"Well, God exists whether you believe in Him or not and He has some answers for your life," Mike told him. "You've given yourself 22 years ... how about giving Him just one week?"

The young man agreed it was worth a try so Mike took him home and left him with copies of tracts, a Bible and *The Late Great Planet Earth*. He was eager to get to his assignment.

The God Squad doesn't know what became of him,

but they do know that the night of his encounter with Mike Phillips, he had more hope of making it than at any other time in his life. He had heard the message of the gospel and God's Word does not return void.

Mike Phillips has a good communication hook-up with the Holy Spirit and he can tell when he's being radioed. Often he feels a quickening of the pulse and a pounding in his chest. When that happens, he knows something's going to pop.

He felt that call one morning on his way to work and later in the day he was to learn what it meant. "Domestic at 34th & Tennyson. Divorcee beaten by boyfriend."

"Before we became Christians," Mike says, "our modus operandi in domestics was to get one of the parties out of the house so we could quiet things down. Often we'd have to take the husband to jail ... or if there weren't justification for that, we'd take the wife to a friend's home or to her parents ... anywhere to split the two apart. Of course, that was only a temporary solution.

"What the couples needed, however, was to sit down with a neutral third party and get to the heart of those problems that erupted in violence.

"So our new approach is to minister to the people together ... sharing with them the Word of God and *He* acts as the neutral party. We have a good relationship with priests and ministers in the area and we ask them to follow up with further counseling. It's been effective. It's rare we're ever called back."

"I don't know what happened," the young man said. "I don't know why I struck her. We used to be so close ... we used to have such good times together."

Both parties, Larry and Jenny, said they were church goers and had often gone together. Larry even said he'd often felt the presence of the Holy Spirit.

"What's the feeling like?" Mike asked, recalling the many times he'd experienced the ecstatic, tingling excitement that made his heart pound.

"It's sort've wierd," Larry said. "It's a cold, scary feeling." He explained that sometimes he'd even heard tapping on the walls. Once he'd even seen Jenny's puppy, hair standing on end, back up against the refrigerator and growl when nothing was there.

"That's not the Holy Spirit," Mike assured him and then asked if the two had been dabbling with such things as ouija boards and witchcraft. Larry told him that Jenny had psychic abilities. "She knows things about people without being told," he said, "and sometimes she can tell what's going to happen before it happens."

"It's a gift from God," Jenny said.

"It's communicating with spirits," Mike told her, "and God forbids such practices." He read from chapters 13 and 18 of Deuteronomy. The young couple was stunned. "I had Bob Frayling with me at the time," Mike recalls, "and he was just a brand-new Christian. He'd never heard of such things as spirits or demons and he was so dumbfounded, his eyes looked like fried eggs."

The counseling session ended with the laying on of hands which Jenny requested. She wanted physical as well as spiritual healing.

"Bob and I stood with Jenny between us," Mike relates, "each with one hand on her head, the other pointed upward. And we prayed. Oh, how we prayed for her deliverance. When we opened our eyes we noted several curious onlookers staring through the windows. They'd just emerged from the bar across the street and it was obvious they couldn't quite believe what they were seeing. Stranger than pink elephants no doubt."

Jenny was healed at that meeting and has since become a radiant Christian. She often helps the God Squad by counseling those despondent people who need an understanding woman's touch.

Many who are ignorant of God's Word on the subject of healing find such accounts difficult to accept. Even those who believe Christ once did those things, doubt man can have the same power today. Yet God's Word states, "... greater works than these shall ye do," and makes it plain the laying on of hands is a method through which healing can be accomplished.

Jenny's healing isn't the only one Mike Phillips has been a party to.

He once felt led to pray for another even though the party himself said he felt just fine and didn't need any sort of cure. But Mike and other members of the God Squad laid hands on him and prayed anyway. The man began to perspire, became sick to his stomach and convulsed for 15 minutes with dry vomiting. Finally he relaxed, then exclaimed ecstatically, "It's gone! For 15 years I've had this sex problem and it plagued me night and day."

That man left rejoicing and thanked God the Holy Smokies had come to his aid. That incident, along with many others, has convinced members of The God Squad that when they're open to receiving calls from the Holy Spirit, anything can happen.

Officer Bill Linebach found that out one night when he heard a report of trouble involving two motorists at gun point. "Even though I was in another section of the city," he relates, "I somehow felt I should go."

And it's lucky for a certain unemployed minister that he did.

The man stood on the steps waving a gun at the motorist who had followed him home. The officer at the scene sent the motorist on his way when Linebach got there and turned his attention to the man holding the gun.

"He threatened to beat me to a pulp," the man said when asked why he'd produced the weapon. "He was so mad I'd cut in ahead of him he tailed me all the way home."

Linebach took charge. "God sent me here as a Christian to tell you you've fallen away from the Lord," he said. "You need to get things squared away with Him."

The man began to weep, said he'd been a minister of a church that had folded, and that he was living a life he was ashamed of. He asked for lenience. Linebach arranged for counseling with another minister who, in turn, led the backslider into a field he'd always been interested in—Christian radio.

How was Linebach able to zero in on the heart of the problem without being told? "The Holy Spirit provided the words," he says. "I didn't know what I was going to say. I just furnished the voice box."

The God Squad identifies itself in a unique way. The men wear small gold fish pins on the necktie of the winter uniform and above the pocket on the summer shirt.

"It took a special dispensation from the Chief of Police to wear this Christian symbol on the summer garb," Mike says. "We can wear anything we want to on our neckties, but the summer outfits don't come with ties and regulations prohibit wearing anything like that. The Chief opposed the idea initially but finally granted permission."

"It lets people who recognize it know they're dealing with Christian officers," the men say with pride. "And it gives us an opportunity to witness to those who ask what it stands for."

The God Squad is currently in the process of organizing a youth center where young people can get together for activity and sharing. Plans are that Christian films will be shown, counselors will offer help to those who request it, and literature, music and testimonies will present the gospel story.

A corporation has been formed, the papers have been drawn up and the search is on for a location. The organization is to be non-profit and tax exempt. The center will be called the COP SHOP. "We decided to use the word *cop*," Mike Phillips says, "because its letters stand for Christ Overcomes Problems."

The symbol will be a police hat and badge with a cross on it.

So the Holy Smokies in Appleton, Wisconsin are on the move. They're doing things cops just don't do and they're getting results cops just don't get. "We've found a new meaning in our work since we've become ministers for the Lord," say the six super troopers in the God Squad. "We used to feel being a cop was the most hopeless job in the world. We've got a new outlook on this business now."

Some say anybody can handle domestics and traffic violations. So what's the big deal? Well, the big deal is the changed life and there are hundreds of those in Appleton.

All Holy Smokey calls aren't initially routine, however. God moves in on heavy stuff, too. Minnesota Smokey John Fitzgerald can testify to that.

Chapter XV

The Outreach

Sherry said she wasn't feeling well when her mother asked if she were coming with her to church. "Just a stomach ache, Mom," she said, hoping to sound both serious and nonchalant. "You go on, I'll be fine."

She stood at the window and watched her mother drive off. Then moving quickly, she donned sneakers, blue jeans and shirt, flung a back pack over her shoulders and left the house. Somewhere out there was a big, beautiful world. Somewhere there was freedom and she would find it. She'd hitchhike. Someone would pick her up . . . someone would take her to where life was fun, or part of the way at least.

She was fourteen years old.

Someday, but not for a long time, she'd let her parents know where she was. She'd tell them she was happy, she was fine. She had her own apartment, she had a job, she was dating this neat guy. But for now she was being smart by disappearing without so much as a farewell note. They'd never let her go if they knew . . . never in a thousand years.

Oh, her parents were OK so far as parents go, but they just didn't understand. She was tired of having them tell her what to do and what time she had to be home whenever she went anywhere. She was old enough to go out with boys but they said she had to wait. Well, she was tired of waiting.

The two men had just been released from the State Penitentiary and were working for a land fill company somewhere in South Dakota. Going straight was a drag. Working for a living was a drag. It definitely wasn't their cup of moonshine. Besides, Saturday was pay day and they were solvent. Why not take their middlin' and head for, say Minneapolis? If they kept it between the ditches, they could easily make it by Sunday morning, even doing double nickles. Chances were they could stir up some excitement in the big city without getting caught. Having graduated from the Joint, they'd learned plenty of things they hadn't tried.

Police Sergeant John Fitzgerald sat at his desk going over monthly reports. Things were quiet but that wasn't unusual for St. Louis Park on a Sunday morning. The suburb was one of the more peaceful residential districts in Minneapolis so far as criminal activities go.

"Anything I can do here, Sergeant?" the rookie asked, hoping to snag an indoor assignment from his supervisor. He hated bugging people with tickets on Sundays.

The sergeant looked up from his papers. "Got to slow things down on 7," he said. "You've got the radar unit in your squad, haven't you?"

"Yes, sir," the rookie said reluctantly, trying to hide the disappointment which registered in his face. He turned to leave.

"Wait a minute, Brad," the sergeant said. He had

sensed the young man's mood and he shoved his papers aside. "I think I'll ride with you this morning."

"Good," the rookie replied, pleased at the prospect of having company even if it was the boss.

They headed on out toward Highway 7.

"You know, Sergeant," the young officer said after having driven in silence for several minutes, "I've been wondering about this kind of work. I like it OK and all that, but just what good do we do? I mean, we write tickets, we arrest people . . . for what? We don't ever change anything."

John Fitzgerald had a ready answer. Even though he'd been on the force for a number of years, he still maintained the enthusiasm of his rookie days. He had not gone sour. "We do a lot of good," he said confidently. "Why just think, for instance, what traffic problems there'd be without us. Maybe it doesn't seem as if writing tickets is important, but just by our presence alone, we prevent a lot of things from happening . . ."

A teenager sped by looking neither left nor right. He was 10 mph over the limit. The rookie looked to his supervisor, caught his affirmative nod, then pushed the accelerator down.

They stopped the boy just as he approached the highway. Brad Stevens got out. He went through the routine preliminaries, then began writing a ticket—one he'd have ignored if his supervisor hadn't been sitting there.

Just then a blue '72 Mustang with South Dakota plates went through a stop sign, rolled out onto the highway and made a U turn. "We'd better go after that one," Fitzgerald said. "Now."

There wasn't time for Brad to finish what he'd started. "You'll have to ride along for a few minutes," he said to the young speeder as he opened the back door of the squad. The boy got in.

When the Mustang was stopped, it was Sergeant Fitzgerald who got out to do the talking. Somehow he didn't like the feel of things. The driver and his companion were too eager to please. Probably hiding something he thought. And the young girl in the back seat. What was she doing there? He noticed her back pack and began to ask questions.

"You guys see that red light back there? Know it's unsafe to make a U turn on a highway like that? Where are you from? Where do you work? What brings you to Minneapolis? Ever been in trouble with the law? Driver's licenses?"

The men apologized for their carelessness. "We were kind've confused, Officer," they said. "Never been here before."

"If you don't mind, we'll run some checks on you."

The men did mind but knew better than to object. They knew the sergeant would find out about their stints in the pen. He did, but he didn't mention it . . . not then. Instead he went back to the questions. "What's the girl doing in the back? Is she a runaway? Did you pick her up? You know if you did and she's a runaway, you're contributing to the delinquency of a minor and you can get yourselves in a bit of trouble."

"We don't want any trouble," they said nervously. "We don't know how old she is. We don't know if she's on the run. We saw her thumbing it so we gave her a lift, that's all."

"Young lady, you come with me," Fitzgerald said, opening the back door.

The girl obeyed. She was pale, frightened, shaking. "Please don't tell my parents," she whispered, trying to hold back the tears.

"Now you fellows, I know about your records, but

I'm not going to detain you further. There aren't any
wants out for you. I'm going to suggest that you head
on home and that you keep the slate clean from here
on out."

The men were relieved. The driver started the en-
gine, cautiously pulled the Mustang back onto the
highway and slowly headed west.

Sergeant Fitzgerald turned to the girl and continued asking questions. She gave her name and age
and admitted she was running away from home.

"Do you love your parents, Sherry?"

"Oh yes, I love them," she said readily.

"Do they love you?"

"Yes, I'm sure of that."

The sergeant thought of his own 14-year-old
daughter and knew the pain he'd feel if she were in
Sherry's place. His voice was kind. "Then why are
you doing this to them?" he asked.

Sherry shook her head. She had no answer. How
could she tell the officer so he'd understand? How
could she explain why she just had to leave home?
How could she tell him what she was searching for?
What words could she use that would make it all
sound sensible?

"I know what you're looking for," John said quietly, as if reading her mind.

The girl looked up at him through her tears. "You
do?" she asked incredulously. "What is it?"

"You're looking for Jesus," came the reply.

Sherry was stunned. She hadn't expected that
from a cop. She'd heard about Jesus all her life. In
fact, she'd once asked Him to come into her heart.
That was a long time ago . . . when she was in 5th
grade. She had meant it then, but somewhere along
the line she had tuned that sort of talk out. But there
was something about this officer which made the talk

sound different. He seemed so positive. Like he wasn't just saying words. And he seemed to care. "Tell me more about it," she said.

And so the Holy Smokey from St. Louis Park did. To her questions of how to have fun without drinking and drugs, he explained that such pleasures were short-lived and led down roads she wouldn't want to take if she knew. To her questions of why parents had to be so strict, he explained that God had placed them in authority over her and that they were obeying Him when they gave her rules to follow. So in disobeying her parents, Sherry was actually disobeying God. That's why she was unhappy. He told her the men with whom she'd hitched a ride had just been released from prison, that their intentions toward her were most likely bad, that perhaps her very life had been in danger. "God sent me here to prevent anything from happening to you, Sherry. He loves you. He cares what happens to you. He must have a very special plan for your life."

Sherry was reunited with her mother who came down to the station immediately after having been called away from church. "It's a miracle," the mother said when she heard the whole story. "Thank God for Christian police officers."

Before they left, Sergeant John Fitzgerald prayed with the two of them and asked Sherry to do three things. "I want you to obey your parents," he said. "I want you to read your Bible and write down all God's promises to you, and I want you to drop me a line now and then . . . let me know how you're doing."

John believes that Sherry could have been raped and murdered. That she could have been buried in that land fill in South Dakota and never been found. He has no way of proving that, of course, but there is no doubt in his mind that God wanted the girl brought home safely, that He sent one of His Holy Smokies to get the job done. "I had no earthly reason to ride with Brad that morning," he says. "The Holy Spirit prompted me to make that decision."

At the time of that incident, Fitzgerald had just been promoted to sergeant. "If it hadn't been for that I wouldn't have been on duty. I don't know if I got a promotion for that reason alone," he says, "but getting it was a miracle in itself and I know God had a hand in it."

It seemed promotions were hard to come by in the St. Louis Park precinct. But John Fitzgerald took the written tests anyway. He passed, one of the top three, and was called in for oral tests. One question asked what the greatest achievement in his life had been. "While I realized becoming a Christian wasn't actually *my* achievement," he relates, "I felt I had an opportunity to testify for my Lord. Besides, it was the most important thing that had ever happened to me so that's the answer I gave."

He was called in for two more orals after that and was asked the same question during each. Not only did he give the same answer, he gave the exact time and date of his conversion. The examiners were dubious. They said they weren't after missionaries, they wanted cops. Could Fitzgerald stand to get his lily white hands dirty? Could he measure up when things got tough? Could he use a gun if necessary or would he just stand there and preach a sermon?

To each question John had a ready answer... one he claims was provided for him by God. "The examiners didn't know it," he says, "but that night was prayer meeting at the church and I had asked my friends to pray for me. Their prayers were answered. I got my promotion."

God's Holy Smokey has had other unique experiences as a police officer, too ... experiences that have convinced him he's where God wants him to be. He stopped a drunken driver one night and had the chance to witness to him about the saving power of Christ. The man had been weaving down the highway when John pulled him over and requested that he blow into the portable breathalizer. "I'm not drunk," the man insisted. "I had one drink and that was just a few minutes ago."

Since the meter will register high if the party has just taken a drink, John decided to wait the recommended 15 minutes and give him another test just to be sure. While he waited, he asked the man about himself. His eyes were watery because he'd been crying, not drinking he said. He was miserable. He owned his own electric contracting business. He had a ranch, a lovely wife, four beautiful children ... everything, but still he wasn't happy. His marriage was breaking up. In fact, right then he was out looking for another woman. "I'm on the skids and I know it," he said.

"At one time my marriage was breaking up, too," Fitzgerald told him. "I went to a counselor who told me it would take a year of therapy to straighten me out. But I surrendered my life to Christ and He straightened out my marriage in two minutes. Claudette and I have been extremely happy ever since."

The second breath test registered in the warning area so John let the man go. Before doing so, however, he gave him a card. "It has the police chapplain's name and number," he said. "Please call him if you need further help."

The chaplain reported later the man called at 2 a.m. that very morning. "The guy was desperate," he said. "I went out there the next day and spent the afternoon with him and his wife. She accepted Christ and the man is seriously considering it."

On another occasion, Fitzgerald brought a young man in for indecent exposure. During the booking process, he contacted the man's community and found he'd been arrested innumerable times for similar incidents. The young man, who gave his name as Terry, said he'd talk to Fitzgerald but not to any other officers. There was something about this sergeant that put him at ease.

When asked how long he'd been exposing himself to young women, he replied that it had been about ten years. To all appearances it looked as if Terry had everything going for him. He was strong and handsome. He was intelligent. He came from a fine family. He was about to graduate from college and with honors. He said he'd gone to counseling sessions and was currently taking a Human Sexuality course in an attempt to understand his problem. "I want help," he said. "It's like this black cloud comes over me and I get an uncontrollable urge to do indecent things."

Sexual deviation wasn't Terry's only problem, however. He was unhappily living with a girl outside of marriage. He drank much too heavily and he was into drugs. As the two men talked, Fitzgerald led the conversation to spiritual matters. Terry said he believed in God. "I was raised a Catholic," he said, "and I went to church every Sunday. I was an altar boy, in fact. I attended a Catholic high school. I know I'm all messed up. I don't set foot inside a church anymore."

"Your problem is sin, Terry," Fitzgerald said, then went on to explain that when God made man, He made him to have fellowship with Him. But man's sin separated him from God and to restore that fellowship, God sent Jesus Christ to redeem man from his sin.

Terry wept softly as John spoke to him then gained control of himself. He'd been distraught. He'd felt hopeless, but now there was reason to be encouraged.

"I assured him," Fitzgerald relates, "that help wasn't 75 counseling sessions down the road. It was just a prayer away."

"I have prayed," Tony said. "Every time I feel this urge coming on I pray."

"Perhaps the reason your prayer isn't answered is that God wants to straighten out your life in all areas. He isn't satisfied just to have you free from your sexual hang-ups. He knows you won't be happy until the other things are taken care of, too. If you're willing to let them all go, He'll help you. There's no question in my mind about that."

Terry left with his spirits having been lifted and he left with hope in his heart. He asked for the sergeant's name. "I'd like to talk to you again sometime," he said.

When John told me the story of Terry, I thought of the time early in my career when I had seen the nude man running the streets in mid-January. While others had laughed, I had felt sick inside. I had wondered how to help a guy like that. Now I know the answer. Holy Smokey John Fitzgerald found the way and that is to minister to such people about sin and salvation.

There's a national organization called Fellowship of Christian Peace Officers which has done much in the way of helping Christian policemen and women throughout the country renew their faith and reach out to others who have become disillusioned with their jobs. The word *peace* instead of *police* [officers] is used since the group's purpose is to serve all men and women connected with law enforcement —highway patrolmen,those in federal agencies and so forth.

When Minneapolis tried to get a chapter off the ground four or five years ago, it failed miserably. But now, thanks to the faith of men like John Fitzgerald and to the testimony of a successful Christ-centered drug rehabilitation center like Midwest Challenge, it's finally becoming a reality.

When the Center first opened its doors, law enforcement officers were skeptical. They said I was crazy. Some said I'd simply figured out a new way to rip people off. They talk differently now and they think differently. Their minds and their hearts are open.

When St. Louis Park tried to generate interest in the organization five years ago, John Fitzgerald was the only one who attended the meeting. Needless to say, the effort was abandoned.

But when the Minneapolis group held its first monthly breakfast meeting early this year, there were five Christian police officers from St. Louis Park in attendance—10% of the number on their roles. That figure is heartening.

"I think the reason we failed initially," John says, "is that we thought of it more as an in-house blessing agency. We were more interested in what we'd get than in what we could do to reach out to others."

I think he's right. Certainly our purpose is to encourage fellow Christian officers, but we're also interested in sharing the gospel message with those outside the organization. And with people who aren't in this business at all.

The group had its organizational dinner at the Radisson Hotel last October with some 65 men and women in attendance. As a result of that meeting, one St. Louis Park policeman has come to know Christ and others have experienced the lift that comes from sharing burdens with praying Christians who care.

Jerry Martin, the new convert in Fitzgerald's precinct, had been eager about the idea from the start. When he first heard about it, he asked for an application form and said he wanted to sign up. He filled out the blanks and when he got to the last question which asked for a personal testimony of faith in Jesus Christ, Jerry, who knew he wasn't a Christian, wrote in "more to follow."

Shortly after that he did surrender his life to Christ; and when the first breakfast meeting was held on January 8 at Uncle John's Pancake House on Highway 7 and Lake Road, Jerry Martin had a testimony to give and he volunteered it.

Another man in attendance at that breakfast had seen the notification of it on the bulletin board at the Eden Prairie station. Feeling it would be what he needed, he came with a burden but with a hope that someone could help him. His wife had announced that morning she was leaving him. "I hope you don't look upon my telling you this as a sign of weakness," he said to the group, "but I don't know where to turn."

The twenty-seven men who were gathered at that meeting listened quietly. Not one of them considered the man weak. They knew his confession had taken great courage . . . that it was a sign of strength. And all of them prayed in earnest that God would mend the rift in his marriage. The man was greatly encouraged.

One officer heard about the organization in a miraculous way and while he couldn't attend the first meeting, he's anxious to become a member.

It happened when John Fitzgerald located the

driver of a car which was illegally parked at City Hall. He noticed an "I Found It" sticker on the bumper; and though he knew what it meant, he asked the driver to explain it. The man readily testified he had found salvation in Jesus Christ. John told him about the new organization. The man in turn gave him the name of an officer friend who, he said, would be very interested. So John gave him a call. Not only was he interested, he was overjoyed. He'd been asking around for just such an organization he said.

"There's no doubt in my mind God parked that car blocking the entrance of City Hall," Fitzgerald says.

The group has already begun an outreach program, and they plan to do more along that line. The kids in Minneapolis, for example, are getting the gospel message with the help of a member from the Canine Squad of all things! And they're loving it. Officer Luke Koerner, an enthusiastic Christian who works with the dogs, is becoming a popular speaker at groups where youngsters gather. He brings his dog with him and while Rex does his act, Luke preaches the word.

Bob Lutz is the president of Minnesota's chapter of Fellowship of Peace Officers. He's an ardent Christian whose main concern is that other officers find the Lord. As a member of the Internal Affairs Unit, Bob investigates situations in which police officers are in trouble . . . some of it serious trouble. He cares about their personal problems and he knows from experience that God has solutions. "We're just getting started," Bob says of the fellowship, "but already we're excited about what's happening. God is definitely moving and we're trusting many souls will be brought to Him."

One by one law officers everywhere are joining

the ranks as ministers in Heaven's Precinct. And slowly but surely the traditional forms of law enforcement are experiencing dramatic changes. Miracles are unfolding. The time will come when all the world will recognize Jesus Christ as Lord and Savior, King of Kings and Prince of Peace. It's going to be a great day and God's Holy Smokies are doing what they can to hasten its arrival.

I'm looking forward with excitement to the future. The story hasn't ended; it's just beginning. I know, as Jerry Martin knew when he completed his application for membership in the Fellowship of Christian Peace Officers, "THERE'S MORE TO FOLLOW."

Some Good Things Are Happening At Midwest Challenge Homes

Dramatic and beautiful changes have been taking place in the lives of many young people since our center began in 1972. Ninety-four percent of the graduates who have come with problems such as narcotic addiction, alcoholism and delinquency have found release and happiness in a new way of living—with Christ. The continued success of this work is made possible through contributions from individuals who are concerned about helping young people gain freedom from enslaving habits. Will you join with us in this work by sending a check?

MIDWEST CHALLENGE
3049 Columbus Ave. So.
Minneapolis, MN 55407
612-825-2466

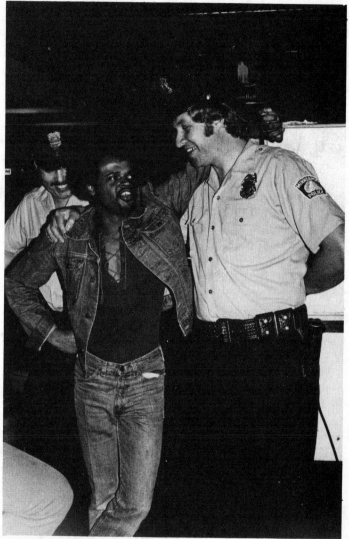

Al Palmquist sharing Christ with a young man who was
in a bar-room fight.